MEI STRUCTURED MATHEMATICS

SECOND EDITION

Mechanics 2

John Berry
Pat Bryden
Ted Graham
Roger Porkess

Series Editor: Roger Porkess

Hodder & Stoughton

Acknowledgements

We are grateful to the following companies, institutions and individuals who have given permission to reproduce photographs in this book. Every effort has been made to trace and acknowledge ownership of copyright. The publishers will be glad to make suitable arrangements with any copyright holders whom it has not been possible to contact.

Colorsport (pages 110 and 116), J Allan Cash Photolibrary (page 1), MC Escher *Waterfall* © 2000 Cordon Arts B.V. – Baarn – Holland, all rights reserved (page 82), Bernard Hinault/Action-Plus (bottom right page 13), Hodder Picture Library (bottom middle page 13), Imperial College (page 153), Emma Lee (page 59), Glyn Kirk/Action-Plus (page 61), Andrew Lambert (top of page 13), Northern Counties Buses (page 53), Dave Thompson/Life File (bottom left page 13), and Neil Tingle/ Action-Plus (pages 103 and 143).

OCR, AQA and Edexcel accept no responsibility whatsoever for the accuracy or method of working in the answers given.

Orders: please contact Bookpoint Ltd, 78 Milton Park, Abingdon, Oxon OX14 4TD. Telephone: (44) 01235 827720, Fax: (44) 01235 400454. Lines are open from 9.00–6.00, Monday to Saturday, with a 24 hour message answering service. Email address: orders@bookpoint.co.uk

British Library Cataloguing in Publication Data
A catalogue record for this title is available from The British Library

ISBN 0340 771 925

First published 1994
Second edition published 2000
Impression number   10 9 8 7 6 5 4 3 2 1
Year   2005 2004 2003 2002 2001 2000

Copyright © 1994, 2000, J S Berry, Pat Bryden, E Graham and Roger Porkess

Typeset by Tech-Set Ltd, Gateshead, Tyne & Wear.
Printed in Great Britain for Hodder & Stoughton Educational, a division of Hodder Headline Plc, 338 Euston Road, London NW1 3BH by J. W. Arrowsmiths, Bristol.

MEI Structured Mathematics

Mathematics is not only a beautiful and exciting subject in its own right but also one that underpins many other branches of learning. It is consequently fundamental to the success of a modern economy.

MEI Structured Mathematics is designed to increase substantially the number of people taking the subject post-GCSE, by making it accessible, interesting and relevant to a wide range of students.

It is a credit accumulation scheme based on 45 hour modules which may be taken individually or aggregated to give Advanced Subsidiary (AS) and Advanced GCE (A Level) qualifications in Mathematics, Further Mathematics and related subjects (like Statistics). The modules may also be used to obtain credit towards other types of qualification.

The course is examined by OCR (previously the Oxford and Cambridge Schools Examination Board) with examinations held in January and June each year.

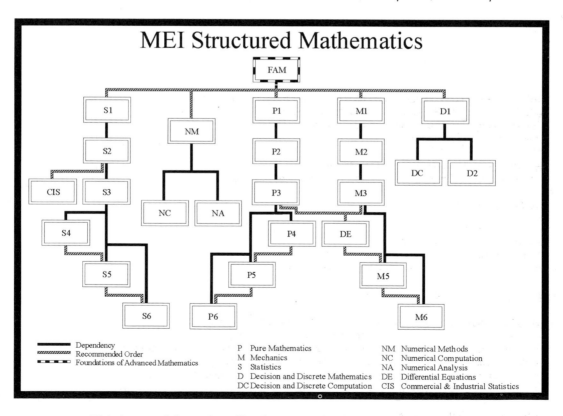

This is one of the series of books written to support the course. Its position within the whole scheme can be seen in the diagram above.

Mathematics in Education and Industry is a curriculum development body which aims to promote the links between Education and Industry in Mathematics at secondary school level, and to produce relevant examination and teaching syllabuses and support material. Since its foundation in the 1960s, MEI has provided syllabuses for GCSE (or O Level), Additional Mathematics and A Level.

For more information about MEI Structured Mathematics or other syllabuses and materials, write to MEI Office, Albion House, Market Place, Westbury, Wiltshire, BA13 3DE.

Introduction

This is the second in a series of books to support the Mechanics modules in MEI Structured Mathematics. They are also suitable for other courses in the subject. Throughout the series emphasis is placed on understanding the basic principles of Mechanics and the process of modelling the real world, rather than on mere routine calculations.

This book builds on the concepts introduced in *Mechanics 1*, giving a deeper treatment of some of the ideas you met there, such as friction and centre of mass. Previous work on forces is applied to pin-jointed structures. The book also introduces a number of new concepts: the rigid body model, energy and momentum.

Some examples of everyday applications are covered in the worked examples in the text, many more in the various exercises. Working through these exercises is an important part of learning the subject. Not only will it help you to appreciate the wide variety of situations that can be analysed using mathematics, it will also build your confidence in applying the techniques you have learnt.

Mechanics is not just a pen-and-paper subject. It is about modelling the real world and this involves observing what is going on around you. This book includes a number of simple experiments and investigations for you to carry out. Make sure you do so; they will really help you. These ideas are also covered in the coursework in the MEI Mechanics 2 module; detailed advice on this is available from the MEI office.

We have used S.I. units throughout the book but have from time to time included examples using other common units for example (mph and knots).

This is the second edition of *Mechanics 2* in this series. We have used much of the previous text and most of the questions. However, there are places where we have rewritten the text, and there are many new questions including some from past examination papers. There is also a new section on using experimental results. Thanks are due to Pat Bryden for her work in preparing the new edition. We would also like to thank all those who have looked through early drafts of the text and made helpful suggestions, particularly Robin Grayson. Finally we would like to thank the various examination boards who have given permission for their past questions to be used in the exercises.

Pat Bryden, Roger Porkess, John Berry and Ted Graham

Contents

00061581190010

A model for friction

Theories do not have to be 'right' to be useful.

Alvin Toffler

This statement about a road accident was offered to a magistrate's court by a solicitor.

'Briefly the circumstances of the accident are that our client was driving his Porsche motor car. He had just left work at the end of the day. He was stationary at the junction with Plymouth Road when a motorcyclist travelling down the Plymouth Road from Tavistock lost control of his motorcycle due to excessive speed and collided with the front offside of our client's motor car.

'The motorcyclist was braking when he lost control and left a 26 metre skid mark on the road. Our advice from an expert witness is that the motorcyclist was exceeding the speed limit of 30 mph.'

❷ It is the duty of a court to decide whether the motorcyclist was innocent or guilty. Is it possible to deduce his speed from the skid mark? Draw a sketch map and make a list of the important factors that you would need to consider when modelling this situation.

A model for friction

Clearly the key information is provided by the skid marks. To interpret it, you need a model for how friction works; in this case between the motorcycle's tyres and the road.

As a result of experimental work, Coulomb formulated a model for friction between two surfaces. The following laws are usually attributed to him.

1 Friction always opposes relative motion between two surfaces in contact.
2 Friction is independent of the relative speed of the surfaces.
3 The magnitude of the frictional force has a maximum which depends on the normal reaction between the surfaces and on the roughness of the surfaces in contact.
4 If there is no sliding between the surfaces

$$F \leqslant \mu R$$

where F is the force due to friction and R is the normal reaction.
μ is called *the coefficient of friction*.
5 When sliding is just about to occur, friction is said to be *limiting* and $F = \mu R$.
6 When sliding occurs $F = \mu R$.

According to Coulomb's model, μ is a constant for any pair of surfaces. Typical values and ranges of values for the coefficient of friction μ are given in this table.

Surfaces in contact	μ
wood sliding on wood	0.2–0.6
metal sliding on metal	0.15–0.3
normal tyres on dry road	0.8
racing tyres on dry road	1.0
sandpaper on sandpaper	2.0
skis on snow	0.02

How fast was the motorcyclist going?

You can now proceed with the problem. As an initial model, you might make the following assumptions:

1 that the road is level;
2 that the motorcycle was at rest just as it hit the car. (Obviously it was not, but this assumption allows you to estimate a minimum initial speed for the motorcycle);

3 that the motorcycle and rider may be treated as a particle, subject to Coulomb's laws of friction with $\mu = 0.8$ (i.e. dry road conditions).

The calculation then proceeds as follows.

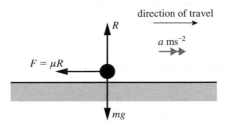

Figure 1.1

Taking the direction of travel as positive, let the motorcycle and rider have acceleration a ms^{-2} and mass m kg. You have probably realised that the acceleration will be negative. The forces (in N) and acceleration are shown in figure 1.1.

Applying Newton's second law:

perpendicular to the road, since there is no vertical acceleration we have

$$R - mg = 0;$$ ①

parallel to the road, there is a constant force $-\mu R$ from friction, so we have

$$-\mu R = ma.$$ ②

Solving for a gives

$$a = -\frac{\mu R}{m} = -\frac{\mu mg}{m} = -\mu g.$$

From ①
$R = mg$

Taking $g = 10$ ms^{-2} and $\mu = 0.8$ gives $a = -8$ ms^{-2}.

The constant acceleration equation

$$v^2 = u^2 + 2as$$

can be used to calculate the initial speed of the motorcycle. Substituting $s = 26$, $v = 0$ and $a = -8$ gives

$$u = \sqrt{2 \times 8 \times 26} = 20.4 \text{ ms}^{-1}.$$

This figure can be converted to miles per hour (using the fact that 1 mile $\approx$ 1600 m):

$$\text{speed} = \frac{20.4 \times 3600}{1600} \text{ mph}$$
$$= 45.9 \text{ mph}.$$

So this first simple model suggests that the motorcycle was travelling at a speed of at least 45.9 mph before skidding began.

How good is this model and would you be confident in offering the answer as evidence in court? Look carefully at the three assumptions. What effect do they have on the estimate of the initial speed?

Modelling with friction

Whilst there is always some frictional force between two sliding surfaces its magnitude is often very small. In such cases we ignore the frictional force and describe the surfaces as *smooth*.

In situations where frictional forces cannot be ignored we describe the surface(s) as *rough*. Coulomb's Law is the standard model for dealing with such cases.

Frictional forces are essential in many ways. For example, a ladder leaning against a wall would always slide if there were no friction between the foot of the ladder and the ground. The absence of friction in icy conditions causes difficulties for road users: pedestrians slip over, cars and motorcycles skid.

Remember that friction always opposes sliding motion.

 In what direction is the frictional force between the back wheel of a cycle and the road?

Historical note

Charles Augustin de Coulomb was born in Angoulême in France in 1736 and is best remembered for his work on electricity rather than for that on friction. The unit for electric charge is named after him.

Coulomb was a military engineer and worked for many years in the West Indies, eventually returning to France in poor health not long before the revolution. He worked in many fields, including the elasticity of metal, silk fibres and the design of windmills. He died in Paris in 1806.

EXAMPLE 1.1

A horizontal rope is attached to a crate of mass 70 kg at rest on a flat surface. The coefficient of friction between the floor and the crate is 0.6. Find the maximum force that the rope can exert on the crate without moving it.

SOLUTION

The forces (in N) acting on the crate are shown in figure 1.2. Since the crate does not move, it is in equilibrium.

Horizontal forces: $T = F$

Vertical forces: $R = mg$

$$= 70 \times 9.8 = 686$$

The law of friction states that:

$$F \leqslant \mu R \text{ for objects at rest.}$$

So in this case $F \leqslant 0.6 \times 686$

$$F \leqslant 411.6$$

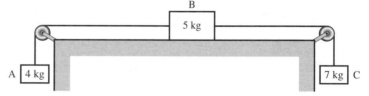

Figure 1.2

The maximum frictional force is 412 N. As the tension in the rope and the force of friction are the only forces which have horizontal components, the crate will remain in equilibrium unless the tension in the rope is greater than 412 N.

EXAMPLE 1.2

Figure 1.3 shows a block of mass 5 kg on a rough table. It is connected by light inextensible strings passing over smooth pulleys to masses of 4 kg and 7 kg which hang vertically. The coefficient of friction between the block and the table is 0.4.

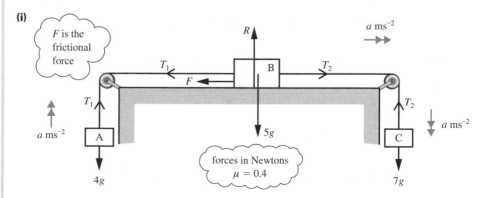

Figure 1.3

(i) Draw a diagram showing the forces acting on the three blocks and the direction of acceleration if the system moves.

(ii) Show that acceleration does take place.

(iii) Find the acceleration of the system and the tensions in the strings.

SOLUTION

(i)

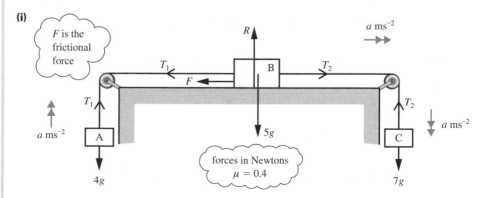

Figure 1.4

If acceleration takes place it is in the direction shown and $a > 0$.

(ii) When the acceleration is $a \, \text{ms}^{-2}$ ($\geqslant 0$), Newton's second law gives

for B, horizontally	$T_2 - T_1 - F = 5a$	①
for A, vertically upwards:	$T_1 - 4g = 4a$	②
for C, vertically downwards:	$7g - T_2 = 7a$	③
Adding ①, ② and ③,	$3g - F = 16a$	④

B has no vertical acceleration so $\quad\quad R = 5g$

The maximum possible value of F is $\mu R = 0.4 \times 5g = 2g$

In ④, a can be zero only if $F = 3g$, so $a > 0$ and sliding occurs.

(iii) When sliding occurs, you can replace F by $\mu R = 2g$

Then ④ gives
$$g = 16a$$
$$a = 0.6125$$

Back-substituting gives $T_1 = 41.65$ and $T_2 = 64.3125$

The acceleration is $0.61 \, \text{ms}^{-2}$ and the tensions are $42 \, \text{N}$ and $64 \, \text{N}$.

EXAMPLE 1.3

Angus is pulling a sledge of mass 12 kg at steady speed across level snow by means of a rope which makes an angle of 20° with the horizontal. The coefficient of friction between the sledge and the ground is 0.15. What is the tension in the rope?

SOLUTION

Since the sledge is travelling at steady speed, the forces acting on it are in equilibrium. They are shown in figure 1.5.

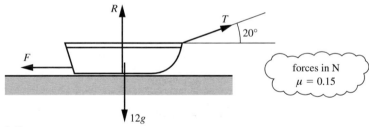

Figure 1.5

Horizontally:
$$T \cos 20° = F$$
$$= 0.15R \quad \longleftarrow \quad F = \mu R \text{ when the sledge slides}$$

Vertically:
$$T \sin 20° + R = 12g$$
$$R = 12 \times 9.8 - T \sin 20°$$

Combining these gives
$$T \cos 20° = 0.15 \, (12 \times 9.8 - T \sin 20°)$$
$$T \, (\cos 20° + 0.15 \sin 20°) = 0.15 \times 12 \times 9.8$$
$$T = 17.8$$

The tension is 17.8 N.

 Notice that the normal reaction is reduced when the rope is pulled in an upwards direction. This has the effect of reducing the friction and making the sledge easier to pull.

EXAMPLE 1.4

A ski slope is designed for beginners. Its angle to the horizontal is such that skiers will either remain at rest on the point of moving or, if they are pushed off, move at constant speed. The coefficient of friction between the skis and the slope is 0.35. Find the angle that the slope makes with the horizontal.

SOLUTION

Figure 1.6 shows the forces on the skier.

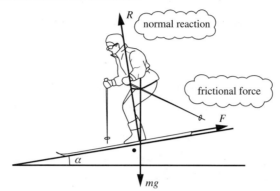

Figure 1.6

The weight mg can be resolved into components $mg \cos \alpha$ perpendicular to the slope and $mg \sin \alpha$ parallel to the slope.

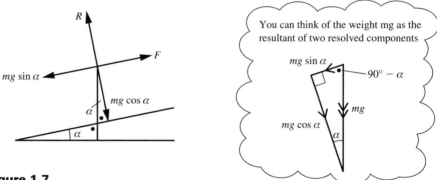

You can think of the weight mg as the resultant of two resolved components

Figure 1.7

Since the skier is in equilibrium (at rest or moving with constant speed) applying Newton's second law:

Parallel to slope: $\qquad mg \sin \alpha - F = 0$

$\qquad\qquad\qquad\qquad \Rightarrow F = mg \sin \alpha$ ①

Perpendicular to slope: $\quad R - mg \cos \alpha = 0$

$\qquad\qquad\qquad\qquad \Rightarrow R = mg \cos \alpha$ ②

In limiting equilibrium or moving at constant speed,

$$F = \mu R$$

$$mg \sin \alpha = \mu \, mg \cos \alpha$$

Substituting for F and R from ① and ②

$$\Rightarrow \qquad \mu = \frac{\sin \alpha}{\cos \alpha} = \tan \alpha.$$

In this case $\mu = 0.35$, so $\tan \alpha = 0.35$ and $\alpha = 19.3°$

Note

1 The result is independent of the mass of the skier. This is often found in simple mechanics models. For example, two objects of different mass fall to the ground with the same acceleration. However when such models are refined, for example to take account of air resistance, mass is often found to have some effect on the result.

2 The angle for which the skier is about to slide down the slope is called the angle of friction. The angle of friction is often denoted by λ (lambda) and defined by $\tan \lambda = \mu$.

When the angle of the slope (α) is equal to the angle of the friction (λ), it is just possible for the skier to stand on the slope without sliding. If the slope is slightly steeper, the skier will slide immediately, and if it is less steep he or she will find it difficult to slide at all without using the ski poles.

EXERCISE 1A

You will find it helpful to draw diagrams when answering these questions.

1 A block of mass 10 kg is resting on a horizontal surface. It is being pulled by a horizontal force T (in N), and is on the point of sliding. Draw a diagram showing the forces acting and find the coefficient of friction when
 (i) $T = 9.8$ **(ii)** $T = 49$.

2 In each of the following situations, use the equation of motion for each object to decide whether the block moves. If so, find the magnitude of the acceleration and if not, write down the magnitude of the frictional force.

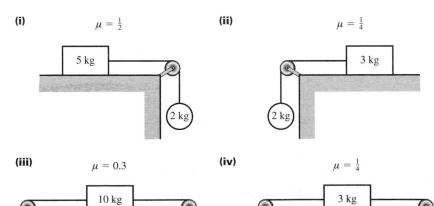

(i) $\mu = \frac{1}{2}$ 5 kg 2 kg

(ii) $\mu = \frac{1}{4}$ 3 kg 2 kg

(iii) $\mu = 0.3$ 10 kg 4 kg 6 kg

(iv) $\mu = \frac{1}{4}$ 3 kg 2 kg 5 kg

3 The brakes on a caravan of mass 700 kg have seized so that the wheels will not turn. What force must be exerted on the caravan to make it move horizontally? (The coefficient of friction between the tyres and the road is 0.7.)

4 A boy slides a piece of ice of mass 100 g across the surface of a frozen lake. Its initial speed is $10\,\text{ms}^{-1}$ and it takes 49 m to come to rest.

(i) Find the deceleration of the piece of ice.

(ii) Find the frictional force acting on the piece of ice.

(iii) Find the coefficient of friction between the piece of ice and the surface of the lake.

(iv) How far will a 200 g piece of ice travel if it, too, is given an initial speed of $10\,\text{ms}^{-1}$?

5 Jasmine is cycling at $12\,\text{ms}^{-1}$ when her bag falls off the back of her cycle. The bag slides a distance of 9 m before coming to rest. Calculate the coefficient of friction between the bag and the road.

6 A box of mass 50 kg is being moved across a room. To help it to slide a suitable mat is placed underneath the box.

(i) Explain why the mat makes it easier to slide the box.

A force of 98 N is needed to slide the mat at a constant velocity.

(ii) What is the value of the coefficient of friction between the box and the floor?

A child of mass 20 kg climbs onto the box.

(iii) What force is now needed to slide the mat at constant velocity?

7 A car of mass 1200 kg is travelling at $30\,\text{ms}^{-1}$ when it is forced to perform an emergency stop. Its wheels lock as soon as the brakes are applied so that they slide along the road without rotating. For the first 40 m the coefficient of friction between the wheels and the road is 0.75 but then the road surface changes and the coefficient of friction becomes 0.8.

(i) Find the deceleration of the car immediately after the brakes are applied.

(ii) Find the speed of the car when it comes to the change of road surface.

(iii) Find the total distance the car travels before it comes to rest.

8 Shona, whose mass is 30 kg, is sitting on a sledge of mass 10 kg which is being pulled at constant speed along horizontal ground by her older brother, Aloke. The coefficient of friction between the sledge and the snow-covered ground is 0.15. Find the tension in the rope from Aloke's hand to the sledge when

(i) the rope is horizontal;

(ii) the rope makes an angle of 30° with the horizontal.

9 In each of the following situations a brick is about to slide down a rough inclined plane. Find the unknown quantity.

(i) The plane is inclined at 30° to the horizontal and the brick has mass 2 kg: find μ.

(ii) The brick has mass 4 kg and the coefficient of friction is 0.7: find the angle of the slope.

(iii) The plane is at 65° to the horizontal and the brick has mass 5 kg: find μ.

(iv) The brick has mass 6 kg and μ is 1.2: find the angle of slope.

10 The diagram shows a boy on a simple playground slide. The coefficient of friction between a typically clothed child and the slide is 0.25 and it can be assumed that no speed is lost when changing direction at B. The section AB is 3 m long and makes an angle of 40° with the horizontal. The slide is designed so that a child, starting from rest, stops at just the right moment of arrival at C.

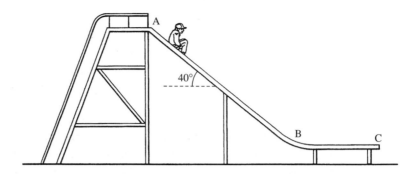

(i) Draw a diagram showing the forces acting on the boy when on the sloping section AB.

(ii) Calculate the acceleration of the boy when on the section AB.

(iii) Calculate the speed on reaching B.

(iv) Find the length of the horizontal section BC.

11 The diagram shows a mop being used to clean the floor. The coefficient of friction between the mop and the floor is 0.3.

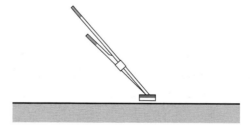

(i) Draw a diagram showing the forces acting on the head of the mop.

In an initial model the weight of the mop is assumed to be negligible.

(ii) Find the angle between the handle and the horizontal when the mop head is moving across the floor at constant velocity. Explain briefly why this angle is independent of how much force is exerted on the mop.

In a more refined model the weight of the head of the mop is taken to be 5 N, but the weight of the handle is still ignored.

(iii) Use this model to calculate the thrust in the handle if it is held at 70° to the horizontal while the head moves at constant velocity across the floor.

(iv) Could the same model be applied to a carpet cleaner on wheels? Explain your reasoning.

12 The coefficient of friction between the skis and an artificial ski slope for learners is 0.3. During a run the angle, α, which the slope makes with the horizontal varies so that initially the skier accelerates, then travels at constant speed and then slows down. What can you say about the values of α in each of these three parts of the run?

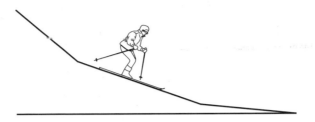

13 The diagram shows a block of mass 0.5 kg resting on a rough inclined plane. The block is attached to a fixed point by a stretched elastic string, parallel to the plane. The coefficient of friction is 0.7 and the angle which the plane makes with the horizontal is given by $\alpha = \arcsin 0.6$.

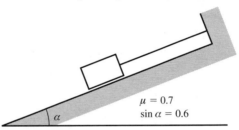

$\mu = 0.7$
$\sin \alpha = 0.6$

(i) Find the tension in the string when the block is on the point of sliding up the plane.

The block is pulled further down the plane from this position so that the tension is greater. It is then released and it slides up the plane for some distance before coming momentarily to rest with the string slack.
(ii) What happens next?

14

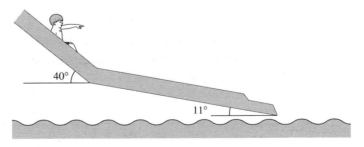

40°

11°

A chute at a water sports centre has been designed so that swimmers first slide down a steep part which is 10 m long and at an angle of 40° to the horizontal. They then come to a 20 m section with a gentler slope, 11° to the horizontal, where they travel at constant speed.

(i) Find the coefficient of friction between a swimmer and the chute.

(ii) Find the acceleration of a swimmer on the steep part.

(iii) Find the speed at the end of the chute of a swimmer who starts at rest. (You may assume that no speed is lost at the point where the slope changes.)

An alternative design of chute has the same starting and finishing points but has a constant gradient.

(iv) With what speed do swimmers arrive at the end of this chute?

15 One winter day, Veronica is pulling a sledge up a hill with slope 30° to the horizontal at a steady speed. The weight of the sledge is 40 N. Veronica pulls the sledge with a rope inclined at 15° to the slope of the hill. The tension in the rope is 24 N.

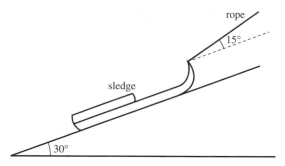

(i) Draw a force diagram showing the forces on the sledge and find the values of the normal reaction of the ground and the frictional force on the sledge.

(ii) Show that the coefficient of friction is slightly more than 0.1.

Veronica stops and when she pulls the rope to start again it breaks and the sledge begins to slide down the hill. The coefficient of friction is now 0.1.

(iii) Find the new value of the frictional force and the acceleration down the slope.

[MEI, adapted]

16 A box of weight 100 N is pulled at steady speed across a rough horizontal surface by a rope which makes an angle α with the horizontal. The coefficient of friction between the box and the surface is 0.4. Assume that the box slides on its underside and does not tip up.

(i) Find the tension in the string when the value of α is
  (a) 10° **(b)** 20° **(c)** 30°

(ii) Find an expression for the value of T for any angle α.

(iii) For what value of α is T a minimum?

1 The sliding ruler

Hold a metre ruler horizontally across your two index fingers and slide your fingers smoothly together, fairly slowly. What happens?

Use the laws of friction to investigate what you observe.

2 Optimum angle
A packing case is pulled across rough ground by means of a rope making an angle θ with the horizontal. Investigate how the tension can be minimised by varying the angle between the rope and the horizontal.

3 Life without friction

Friction forces are essential in many real situations, so life without friction might be rather difficult. Could you survive without friction?

Coulomb's Law

1 The frictional force, F, between two surfaces is given by

$F < \mu R$ when there is no sliding except in limiting equilibrium

$F = \mu R$ in limiting equilibrium

$F = \mu R$ when sliding occurs

where R is the normal reaction of one surface on the other and μ is the coefficient of friction between the surfaces.

2 The frictional force always acts in the direction to oppose sliding.

3 Remember that the value of the normal reaction is affected by a force which has a component perpendicular to the direction of sliding.

2 Using experimental results

One must learn by doing the thing; though you think you know it, you have no certainty until you try.

Sophocles

Using an experiment to test a model

A mathematical model is a model of a situation in the real world and so needs testing back in the real world. This chapter is about obtaining and interpreting experimental results in the light of a model.

Here is an experiment you can do to investigate Coulomb's model of friction for a block in contact with a plane surface. Set up the apparatus as shown in figure 2.1 and use it in two ways.

(i) To find the value of μ when the block is on the point of moving.

(ii) To find the value of μ when the block is moving.

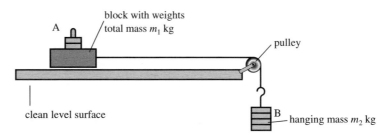

Figure 2.1

(i) STATIC FRICTION

Carefully adjust the weights until the block just begins to slide when you touch it very gently. Calculate the frictional force and the coefficient of friction.

 Is it possible that the block will stay put if you add a little more to B? What happens if you then displace it? What conclusions can you draw?

(ii) DYNAMIC FRICTION

Now adjust the weights so that the block slides. Time it over a measured distance starting from rest and calculate its acceleration. Draw a diagram to show the forces acting on A and B and write down their equations of motion.

Use your equations to calculate the friction force acting on the block and hence work out a value for the coefficient of sliding friction, μ.

Would you expect to obtain the same answer on repeating the experiment

(a) with the same weights?   (b) with different weights?

The answers to both these questions depend on the extent to which you can rely on the accuracy of your measurements. With different weights, there is also the possibility that μ might be different at different speeds.

Planning an experiment

Clearly one set of results is not sufficient to test a model or to obtain a reliable estimate for μ. To test a model you need to plan an experiment carefully, bearing in mind the modelling assumptions and the equations you will need to analyse the results.

? What modelling assumptions do you need to make to investigate dynamic friction using the apparatus in figure 2.1?

Assuming that the pulley is light and smooth, the string is light and inextensible and that there is no air resistance, the forces acting and the acceleration are as shown.

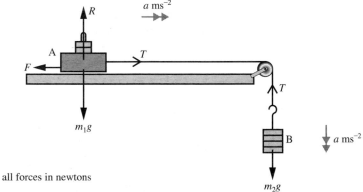

all forces in newtons

Figure 2.2

The equations of motion are:

horizontally for A	$T - F = m_1 a$
vertically for B	$m_2 g - T = m_2 a$
Adding gives	$m_2 g - F = (m_1 + m_2) a$ ①

Vertically for A, $R = m_1 g$ and assuming Coulomb's law, $F = \mu R = \mu m_1 g$.

Substituting in equation ① $m_2 g - \mu m_1 g = (m_1 + m_2) a$

For constant a, the distance, s metres, travelled from rest in t seconds is $s = \frac{1}{2} a t^2$

Substituting for a $m_2 g - \mu m_1 g = (m_1 + m_2)\dfrac{2s}{t^2}$ ②

It is a good idea to keep the number of variables as small as possible and this can be done if you keep $m_1 + m_2$ constant by moving weights between A and B.

Suppose you choose to arrange for the total mass $m_1 + m_2$ to be 0.5 kg and measure the time over a distance $s = 0.7$ m. Then $m_2 = 0.5 - m_1$ and equation ② becomes

$$(0.5 - m_1 - \mu m_1)\, g = \dfrac{0.7}{t^2}$$

Using 9.8 ms^{-2} for g and dividing by 0.7 $\Rightarrow \dfrac{1}{t^2} = 7 - 14(1 + \mu)\, m_1$

Now, assuming μ does not vary, you have only two variables t and m_1 and so you can graph your results. But first consider how accurately you can measure t and m_1. For present purposes assume that stopwatches are the only available timing devices so t is the most difficult to measure.

When several people measure the time with a stopwatch you do not expect them all to obtain the same answer. Why is this? What can you do about it?

Variation in measurements

Two students, P and Q, repeated the experiment keeping the total mass of A and B at a constant 0.5 kg. The table shows the results when they took three measurements of the time to slide 0.7 m from rest for each of six different values of m_1. Look carefully at the figures.

Mass m_1 (kg)	P's times (s)			Q's times (s)			Mean	Min.	Max.
0.05	0.38	0.39	0.38	0.42	0.43	0.43	0.41	0.38	0.43
0.1	0.41	0.43	0.42	0.48	0.45	0.47	0.44	0.41	0.48
0.15	0.48	0.45	0.47	0.50	0.51	0.50	0.49	0.45	0.51
0.2	0.52	0.53	0.55	0.57	0.54	0.92*	0.54	0.52	0.57
0.25	0.61	0.61	0.63	0.64	0.66	0.65	0.63	0.61	0.66
0.3	0.72	0.75	0.74	0.77	0.79	0.79	0.76	0.72	0.79
0.35	1.04	1.05	1.06	1.10	1.08	1.09	1.07	1.04	1.10

You will always find some variation in results. This is known as *random variation*. It is the sort of variation you might experience if you step on your bathroom scales a few times. To allow for random variation it is best to take several measurements.

Looking at the table, you might notice that Q's measurements tend to be higher than P's. If someone makes the same error each time this leads to *systematic variation* in their results. You can't tell from these results whether P's or Q's or both sets of measurements suffer from systematic variation.

❓ What is most likely to cause systematic variations in this experiment?

Systematic variation can be minimised by using several timers, though this won't allow for them all erring in the same direction.

❓ One of Q's times (0.92 s for 0.2 kg) is an *outlier* as it differs a great deal from the other times for the same mass. How could this happen? How can you justify ignoring it? Can you always ignore outliers?

The last three columns show the mean time for each mass and also the maximum and minimum measurements. They can be used to determine *error bounds* for the time.

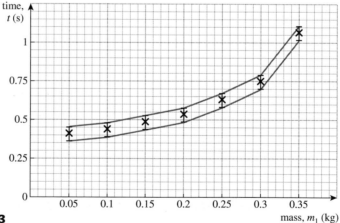

Figure 2.3

Figure 2.3 is a graph of t against m_1 showing the maximum and minimum values of t as *error bars*. m_1 is plotted using the horizontal axis because it is the *independent variable*.

You expect the graph for t to be somewhere between the grey lines. But it is difficult to check the model using this graph. There are many curves whose equations might fit.

Comparing with the model

There are two other methods for processing the data. One is to work with the data and the other is to try to draw a graph which should give a straight line.

WORKING WITH THE DATA

Using the values for m_1 and the last three columns for t to calculate possible values of μ gives the table below. The negative values are impossible so these figures give $0 \leqslant \mu \leqslant 1.9$ with an average of about 0.28.

Mass m_1 (kg)	Mean time (s)	μ	Min. time (s)	μ	Max. time (s)	μ
0.05	0.41	0.29	0.38	−0.89	0.43	1.27
0.1	0.44	0.31	0.41	−0.25	0.48	0.90
0.15	0.49	0.31	0.45	−0.02	0.51	0.50
0.2	0.54	0.28	0.52	0.18	0.58	0.44
0.25	0.63	0.29	0.61	0.23	0.67	0.36
0.3	0.76	0.25	0.72	0.21	0.79	0.29
0.35	1.07	0.25	1.04	0.24	1.10	0.26

 What reason can you give for the negative values obtained for μ?

USING A STRAIGHT LINE

There are a lot of figures in method 1 and you might find it difficult to get an overall view. Often it is better to try to draw a straight line graph. This is one way to do it.

Compare the model with $y = mx + c$. The mass is the independent variable so you want this to be x. The equation for the model can be written as

$$\frac{1}{t^2} = -14\,(1 + \mu)\,m_1 + 7$$

Using y for $\dfrac{1}{t^2}$: $\qquad y = \qquad mx \qquad + c$

$-14\,(1 + \mu)$ is the gradient m, and $c = 7$.

So plot the reciprocal of (time)^2 against mass. If the model is correct, your graph should be a straight line with a gradient of $-14\,(1 + \mu)$ passing through the point $(0, 7)$.

The values of $\dfrac{1}{t^2}$ are shown in the table.

Mass m_1	$\dfrac{1}{t^2}$		
	Mean	Max.	Min.
0.05	6.1	6.9	5.4
0.1	5.1	6.0	4.3
0.15	4.3	4.9	3.8
0.2	3.4	3.7	3.0
0.25	2.5	2.7	2.2
0.3	1.7	1.9	1:6
0.35	0.9	0.9	0.8

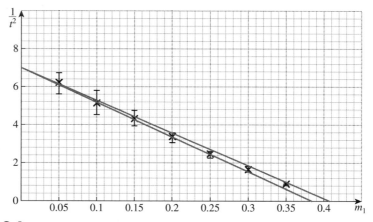

Figure 2.4

The points on the graph are roughly in a straight line which supports Coulomb's model.

You can draw two lines through the point $(0, 7)$ to pass inside the error bars, one giving the greatest gradient and one the least. These give $17.3 \leqslant 14\,(1 + \mu) \leqslant 18.4$, so $0.23 \leqslant \mu \leqslant 0.32$. The mean of the error bounds for μ is 0.28, so the experiment gives a coefficient of friction of about 0.28 ± 0.05.

 Why does this method give smaller error bounds than method 1?

When your experiment differs from the model you need to review the situation. Are the experimental measurements biased? Is the model inappropriate? Or perhaps both of these are possible? In this case, the data could be inaccurate because stopwatches were used.

What effect does squaring t have on possible errors? Which other measurements could also show variation?

ACTIVITY   Carry out a similar experiment, in a group if possible. Before you start, decide how you can minimise errors and prepare a data collection sheet.

Errors related to significant figures and decimal places

The above analysis assumes that the masses are accurate, but they might not be. You could try weighing a number of masses on a sensitive balance to find out.

Suppose a mass labelled 50 g is correct to the nearest gram. This means that in kilograms it is correct to 3 decimal places and should really be written as 0.050 kg.

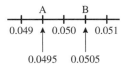

Figure 2.5

The diagram shows a scale of measurements correct to 3 decimal places. Any measurement between A, at $0.050 - 0.0005$, and B, at $0.050 + 0.0005$, is corrected to 0.050. The measurements 0.0495 and 0.0505 are usually corrected upwards. So the error bounds for the mass m kg are given by $0.0495 \leqslant m < 0.0505$.

These error bounds would hardly show on a graph so, in this case, the omission of error bounds for m_1 would be justified.

When the time is written to 2 decimal places, a measurement of 0.44 seconds satisfies the inequality $0.435 \leqslant t < 0.445$ and corresponding error bounds for $\frac{1}{t^2}$ are 5.285 and 5.050. These lie well within the error bounds given by the minimum and maximum values of t^2 in the second row of the table for figure 2.4 (6.0 and 4.3). There is no point in using more than 2 significant figures for t or $\frac{1}{t^2}$ when the variation in the measurements is so large. Similarly, it is pointless to give the coefficient of friction correct to more than 2 significant figures.

EXAMPLE 2.1   A model for the time (in seconds) of swing of a clock pendulum is $T = 2\pi\sqrt{\frac{l}{g}}$. It is known that the value of g where the clock might be used lies within the range 9.81 ± 0.02 and the length l m of the pendulum is measured as 1.00 m correct to 2 decimal places.

(i)   Write down an inequality satisfied by the length of the pendulum.

(ii) Find limits for the time of swing of the pendulum.

(iii) The time of swing should be 2 s for the clock to keep correct time. In the extreme case, how fast will it be after 10 hours?

SOLUTION

(i)   The length lies between $(1.00 - 0.005)$ m and $(1.00 + 0.005)$ m.

$$0.995 \leqslant l < 1.005 \longleftarrow$$

Anything in this range corrects to 1.00

(ii) To find the minimum value of T, use the least value of l and the greatest value of g.

$$T_{min} = 2\pi \sqrt{0.995/9.83}$$
$$= 1.999$$

You get a smaller answer by dividing by a larger value

To find the maximum value of T, use the greatest value of l and the least value of g.

$$T_{max} = 2\pi \sqrt{1.005/9.79}$$
$$= 2.013$$

$T \neq 1.999$ or 2.013 because $g \neq 9.83$ and $l \neq 1.005$

So the limits for the time of the swing are $1.999 < T < 2.013$.

(iii) The clock gains time if the pendulum swings too quickly and it keeps the right time if a half swing takes a second.

The extreme case is $T_{min} = 1.999$ s when a half swing takes 0.9995 s.

Number of half swings per second $= \dfrac{1}{0.9995}$

Number in 10 hours $\qquad = \dfrac{1}{0.9995} \times 36\,000 = 36\,018$

This pendulum counts out 18 extra seconds in 10 hours, so the clock is 18 seconds fast.

Percentage error

If the clock in the example above gained 18 seconds in 1 hour, rather than 10, it would be much less satisfactory. One way of assessing the relative magnitude of an error is to calculate the percentage error.

The percentage error of a value x relative to a value y is $\dfrac{(x - y)}{y} \times 100\%$.

The percentage error for the fast clock relative to an accurate one is

$$\frac{36\,018 - 36\,000}{36\,000} \times 100\% = 0.05\%.$$

1 Write down an inequality satisfied by the given quantity in each of the following cases.
   (i) The diameter, d cm, of a ball is 2.4 cm, to the nearest millimetre.
   (ii) The mass, M kg, of a van is 4100 kg, to the nearest 10 kg.
   (iii) The time, t minutes, to walk around a park is 54 minutes, correct to the nearest 2 minutes.

2 The variables x and y satisfy the inequalities $8.5 \leqslant x < 9.5$ and $0.05 \leqslant y < 0.15$. Calculate suitable inequalities for

   (i) $x + y$ **(ii)** xy **(iii)** $x - y$ **(iv)** $\dfrac{x}{y}$.

3 A coach passenger noted that the driver's speedometer remained at $110 \, \text{km h}^{-1}$ for 15 minutes, both correct to 2 significant figures.
   (i) Calculate the distance travelled using the figures given.
   (ii) Calculate the limits between which the distance must lie.
   (iii) State how many significant figures you can be *sure* of in quoting the distance travelled.
   (iv) What would be a *reasonable rounded-off value* for the distance?

4 When Alan travels from Oxford to Bristol he travels 115 km in 125 minutes (both correct to 3 significant figures).
   (i) Calculate his average speed in km h^{-1} using the given values.
   (ii) Write down inequalities for his distance s km and his time t minutes.
   (iii) Calculate error bounds for his average speed.
   (iv) How many significant figures is it sensible to use for Alan's average speed?

5 Charlie wants to find the depth of a well by dropping a stone down it. She estimates that the stone takes 2.5 s to reach the bottom and she assumes a constant acceleration of $9.8 \, \text{ms}^{-2}$.
   (i) Calculate the depth of the well using Charlie's figures.
   (ii) The time is correct to 2 significant figures and the bounds for the acceleration are 9.79 and 9.81. Calculate upper and lower limits for your answer to part (i).
   (iii) What is a sensible value for Charlie to use?

   In fact the well is 25 m deep to the nearest metre.
   (iv) Explain why even Charlie's lowest estimate is too high.

6 In an experiment to estimate g, a stone is dropped from a window, falling through a height measured as 4.3 m. On one occasion, the time to fall is found to be 1 s.
   (i) Calculate an estimate of g based on these figures. Do you consider this method of estimating g to be:
   (a) accurate   **(b)** reliable?
   (ii) Given that the height could be in error by up to 1 cm, and the time by 0.1 s, find the upper and lower bounds for the estimate of g according to these figures. Comment on your responses to part (i) in the light of these answers.

7 The value of g depends on latitude because the earth is rotating and also because it is not a perfect sphere. It also depends on the height of a point and, to a lesser extent, the terrain beneath it. This formula gives g ms^{-2} at latitude $\theta°$ N and height h m above sea level.

$$g = 9.806\,08 - 0.0257 \cos 2\theta - 0.000\,003h$$

(i) Calculate the values of g correct to 4 significant figures
   (a) on a beach at the equator;
   (b) at the top of Ben Nevis (56.76° N, 1343 m);
   (c) on Yes Tor (50.69° N, 618 m).

(ii) How high should you be at 51° N to make a difference to the fourth significant figure?

(iii) Calculate the value of g where you are.

8 The Highway Code quotes the following figures for typical stopping distances. The initial speed is u mph, with corresponding stopping distance d metres.

u mph	20	30	40	50	60	70
d m	12	23	36	53	73	96

These figures can be simulated by the formula

$$d = 0.3u + 0.015u^2 \text{ (thinking distance + braking distance)}$$
$$d = 0.015u(20 + u)$$

(i) Verify that this formula does give approximately the right values for d for these values of u.

In parts (ii) and (iii) use the formula above as the basis for all your calculations.

(ii) The only legal requirement for the accuracy of a speedometer is that it should register 30 mph with a maximum error of 10% (i.e. when the true speed lies between 27 and 33 mph). Calculate the braking distances corresponding to these extremes and the percentage error in each case relative to the value for 30 mph.

(iii) Repeat these calculations for 10% errors in recorded speeds of 70 mph and 100 mph.

(iv) Comment on the significance of your results in part (iii) for the design specification of a speedometer.

9 (i) Plot a velocity–time graph to show the progress of a vehicle which starts from rest with a constant acceleration of 5 ms^{-2} for 10 s, then proceeds at constant speed for 20 s, and finally slows to rest, again at 5 ms^{-2}.

(ii) In fact the original figures were accurate only to the nearest integer. Add to your graph the two lines which represent the two extreme cases for the figures quoted (i.e. where the distances travelled are greatest and least).

(iii) Calculate the distance travelled in all three cases.

(iv) Calculate the percentage error (relative to the value for the original figures) for the greatest and least distances obtained and compare this with the percentage error allowed for in the original figures.

1 **Using a model**

When planning an experiment, take into account the model's assumptions and the equations to be used.

2 **Variation in experimental results**

- Allow for *random variation* by repeating measurements and using an average and range.
- Be aware of possible *systematic errors* and take steps to minimise these.
- When possible, choose variables so that data can be checked using a straight line graph.

3 **Accuracy of given measurements**

A value v given as 23.4 correct to 3 significant figures lies between $23.4 - 0.05$ and $23.4 + 0.05$. i.e. $23.35 \leqslant v < 23.45$.

The error bounds use one more place than the given value.

4 **Percentage error**

The percentage error of a value x relative to a value y is

$$\frac{(x - y)}{y} \times 100\%$$

3

Moments of forces

Give me a firm place to stand and I will move the earth.

Archimedes

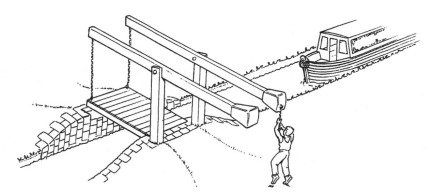

Figure 3.1

The illustration shows a swing bridge over a canal. It can be raised to allow barges and boats to pass. It is operated by hand, even though it is very heavy. How is this possible?

The bridge depends on the turning effects or *moments* of forces. To understand these you might find it helpful to look at a simpler situation.

Two children sit on a simple see-saw, made of a plank balanced on a fulcrum as in figure 3.2. Will the see-saw balance?

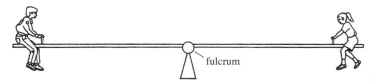

fulcrum

Figure 3.2

If both children have the same mass and sit the same distance from the fulcrum, then you expect the see-saw to balance.

Now consider possible changes to this situation:

(i) If one child is heavier than the other then you expect the heavier one to go down;
(ii) If one child moves nearer the centre you expect that child to go up.

You can see that both the weights of the children and their distances from the fulcrum are important.

What about this case? One child has mass 35 kg and sits 1.6 m from the fulcrum and the other has mass 40 kg and sits on the opposite side 1.4 m from the fulcrum (see figure 3.3).

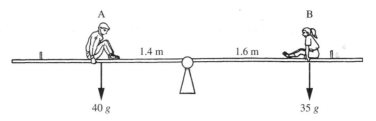

Figure 3.3

Taking the products of their weights and their distances from the fulcrum, gives

A: $40g \times 1.4 = 56\,g$

B: $35g \times 1.6 = 56\,g$

So you might expect the see-saw to balance and this indeed is what would happen.

Rigid bodies

Until now the particle model has provided a reasonable basis for the analysis of the situations you have met. In examples like the see-saw however, where turning is important, this model is inadequate because the forces do not all act through the same point.

In such cases you need the *rigid body model* in which an object, or *body*, is recognised as having size and shape, but is assumed not be deformed when forces act on it.

Suppose that you push a tray lying on a smooth table with one finger so that the force acts parallel to one edge and through the centre of mass (figure 3.4).

Figure 3.4

The particle model is adequate here: the tray travels in a straight line in the direction of the applied force.

If you push the tray equally hard with two fingers as in figure 3.5, symmetrically either side of the centre of mass, the particle model is still adequate.

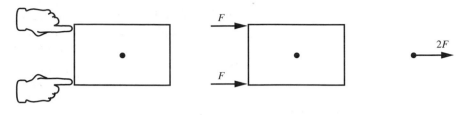

Figure 3.5

However, if the two forces are not equal or are not symmetrically placed, or as in figure 3.6 are in different directions, the particle model cannot be used.

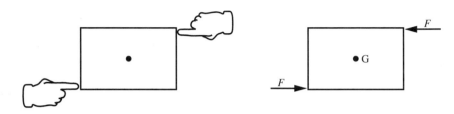

Figure 3.6

The resultant force is now zero, since the individual forces are equal in magnitude but opposite in direction. What happens to the tray? Experience tells us that it starts to rotate about G. How fast it starts to rotate depends, among other things, on the magnitude of the forces and the width of the tray. The rigid body model allows you to analyse the situation.

Moments

In the example of the see-saw we looked at the product of each force and its distance from a fixed point. This product is called the *moment* of the force about the point.

The see-saw balances because the moments of the forces on either side of the fulcrum are the same magnitude and in opposite directions. One would tend to make the see-saw turn clockwise, the other anti-clockwise. By contrast, the moments about G of the forces on the tray in the last situation do not balance. They both tend to turn it anticlockwise, so rotation occurs.

Conventions and units

The moment of a force F about a point O is defined by

$$\text{moment} = Fd$$

where d is the perpendicular distance from the point O to the line of action of the force (figure 3.7).

(i)

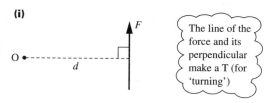

Figure 3.7

In two dimensions, the sense of a moment is described as either positive (anticlockwise) or negative (clockwise) as shown in figure 3.8.

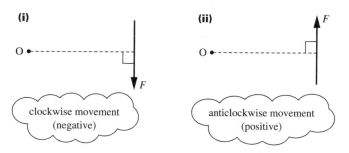

Figure 3.8

If you imagine putting a pin at O and pushing along the line of *F*, your page would turn clockwise for (i) and anticlockwise for (ii).

In the S.I. system the unit for moment is the newton metre (Nm), because a moment is the product of a force, the unit of which is the newton, and distance, the unit of which is the metre.

Remember that moments are always taken about a point and you must always specify what that point is. A force acting through the point will have no moment about that point because in that case $d = 0$.

Figure 3.9 shows two tools for undoing wheel nuts on a car. Discuss the advantages and disadvantages of each.

(i)   **(ii)**

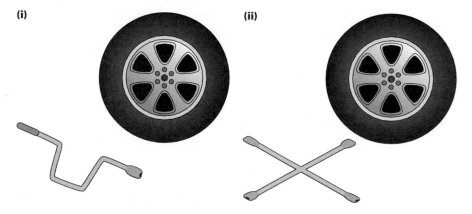

Figure 3.9

When using the spider wrench (the tool with two 'arms'), you apply equal and opposite forces either side of the nut. These produce moments in the same direction. One advantage of this method is that there is no resultant force and hence no tendency for the nut to snap off.

Couples

Whenever two forces of the same magnitude act in opposite directions along different lines, they have a zero resultant force, but do have a turning effect. In fact the moment will be Fd about any point, where d is the perpendicular distance between the forces. This is demonstrated in figure 3.10.

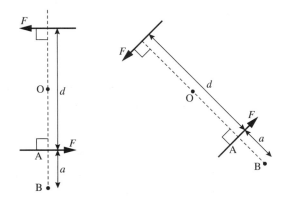

Figure 3.10

In each of these situations:

Moment about O $\qquad F\dfrac{d}{2} + F\dfrac{d}{2} = Fd$ ◄—— anticlockwise is positive

Moment about A $\qquad\qquad 0 + Fd = Fd$

Moment about B $\qquad -aF + (a + d)\,F = Fd$

Any set of forces like these with a zero resultant but a non-zero total moment is known as a couple. The effect of a couple on a rigid body is to cause rotation.

Equilibrium revisited

In *Mechanics 1* we said that an object is in equilibrium if the resultant force on the object is zero. This definition is adequate provided all the forces act through the same point on the object. However, we are now concerned with forces acting at different points, and in this situation even if the forces balance there may be a resultant moment.

Figure 3.11 shows a tray on a smooth surface being pushed equally hard at opposite corners.

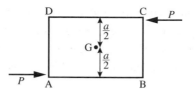

Figure 3.11

The resultant force on the tray is clearly zero, but the resultant moment about its centre point, G, is

$$P \times \frac{a}{2} + P \times \frac{a}{2} = Pa.$$

The tray will start to rotate about its centre and so it is clearly not in equilibrium.

Note

You could have taken moments about any of the corners, A, B, C or D, or any other point in the plane of the paper and the answer would have been the same, *Pa* anticlockwise.

So we now tighten our mathematical definition of equilibrium to include moments. For an object to remain at rest (or moving at constant velocity) when a system of forces is applied, both the resultant force and the total moment must be zero.

To check that an object is in equilibrium under the action of a system of forces, you need to check two things:

(i) that the resultant force is zero;

(ii) that the resultant moment about any point is zero. (You only need to check one point.)

EXAMPLE 3.1

Two children are playing with a door. Kerry tries to open it by pulling on the handle with a force 50 N at right angles to the plane of the door, at a distance 0.8 m from the hinges. Peter pushes at a point 0.6 m from the hinges, also at right angles to the door and with sufficient force just to stop Kerry opening it.

(i) What is the moment of Kerry's force about the hinges?

(ii) With what force does Peter push?

(iii) Describe the resultant force on the hinges.

Figure 3.12

SOLUTION

Looking down from above, the line of the hinges becomes a point, H. The door opens clockwise. Anticlockwise is taken to be positive.

(i)

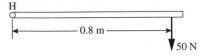

Figure 3.13

Kerry's moment about H $= -50 \times 0.8$
$$= -40 \, \text{Nm}$$

The moment of Kerry's force about the hinges is $-40 \, \text{Nm}$.
(Note that it is a clockwise moment and so negative.)

(ii)

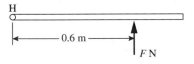

Figure 3.14

Peter's moment about $H = +F \times 0.6$

Since the door is in equilibrium, the total moment on it must be zero, so

$$F \times 0.6 - 40 = 0$$
$$F = \frac{40}{0.6}$$
$$= 66.7$$

Peter pushes with a force of $66.7 \, \text{N}$.

(iii) Since the door is in equilibrium the overall resultant force on it must be zero.

All the forces are at right angles to the door, as shown in the diagram.

Figure 3.15

Resolve $\perp$ to door

$$R + 50 = 66.7$$
$$R = 16.7$$

The reaction at the hinge is a force of $16.7 \, \text{N}$ in the same direction as Kerry is pulling.

Note

The reaction force at a hinge may act in any direction, according to the forces elsewhere in the system. A hinge can be visualised in cross section as shown in figure 3.16. If the hinge is well oiled, and the friction between the inner and outer parts is negligible, the hinge cannot exert any moment. In this situation the door is said to be 'freely hinged'.

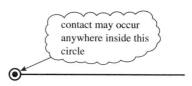

contact may occur anywhere inside this circle

Figure 3.16

EXAMPLE 3.2

The diagram shows a man of weight 600 N standing on a footbridge that consists of a uniform wooden plank just over 2 m long of weight 200 N. Find the reaction forces exerted on each end of the plank.

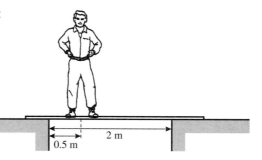

2 m

0.5 m

Figure 3.17

SOLUTION

The diagram shows the forces acting on the plank.

For equilibrium both the resultant force and the total moment must be zero.

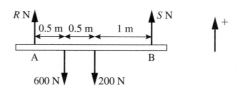

R N S N

0.5 m   0.5 m   1 m

A   B

600 N   200 N

Figure 3.18

As all the forces act vertically we have

$$R + S - 800 = 0 \qquad \qquad \text{①}$$

Taking moments about the point A gives

$$(\curvearrowleft) \qquad R \times 0 - 600 \times 0.5 - 200 \times 1 + S \times 2 = 0 \qquad \text{②}$$

From equation ② $S = 250$ and so equation ① gives $R = 550$.

The reaction forces are 250 N at A and 550 N at B.

Note

1 You cannot solve this problem without taking moments.
2 You can take moments about any point and can, for example, show that by taking moments about B you get the same answer.
3 The whole weight of the plank is being considered to act at its centre.
4 When a force acts through the point about which moments are being taken, its moment about that point is zero.

Levers

A lever can be used to lift or move a heavy object using a relatively small force. Levers depend on moments for their action.

Two common lever configurations are shown below. In both cases a load W is being lifted by an applied force F, using a lever of length l. The calculations assume equilibrium.

Case 1

The fulcrum is at one end of the lever, figure 3.19.

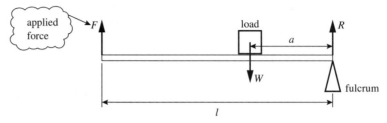

Figure 3.19

Taking moments about the fulcrum

$(\curvearrowright)$ $$F \times l - W \times a = 0$$

$$F = W \times \frac{a}{l}$$

Since a is much smaller than l, the applied force F is much smaller than the load W.

Case 2

The fulcrum is within the lever, figure 3.20.

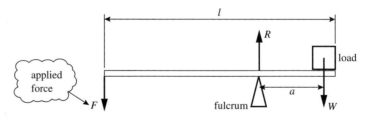

Figure 3.20

Taking moments about the fulcrum

$(\curvearrowleft)$ $$F \times (l - a) - W \times a = 0$$

$$F = W \times \frac{a}{l - a}$$

Provided that the fulcrum is nearer the end with the load, the applied force is less than the load.

These examples also indicate how to find a single force equivalent to two parallel forces. The force equivalent to *F* and *W* should be equal and opposite to *R* and with the same line of action.

❓ Describe the single force equivalent to *P* and *Q* in each of these cases.

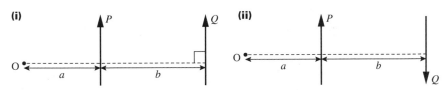

Figure 3.21

In each case state its magnitude and line of action.

❓ How do you use moments to open a screw-top jar?
Why is it an advantage to press hard when it is stiff?

1 In each of the situations shown below, find the moment of the force about the point and state whether it is positive (anticlockwise) or negative (clockwise).

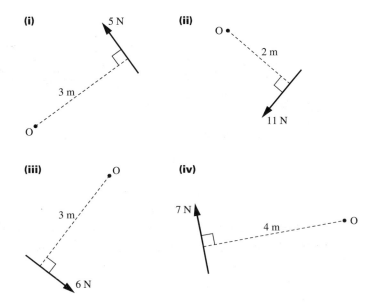

2 The situations below involve several forces acting on each object. For each one, find the total moment.

(i)

(ii)

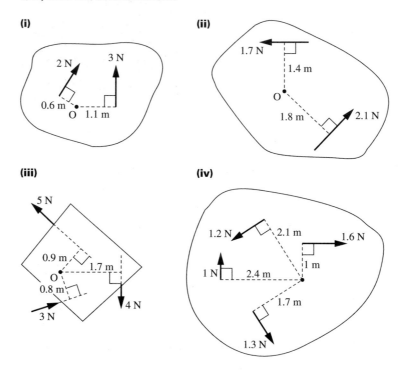

(iii)

(iv)

3 A uniform horizontal bar of mass 5 kg has length 30 cm and rests on two vertical supports, 10 cm and 22 cm from its left-hand end. Find the magnitude of the reaction force at each of the supports.

4 Find the reaction forces on the hi-fi shelf shown below. The shelf itself has weight 25 N and its centre of mass is midway between A and D.

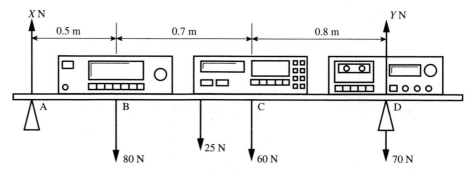

5 The diagram shows a motorcycle of mass 250 kg, and its rider whose mass is 80 kg. The centre of mass of the motorcycle lies on a vertical line midway between its wheels. When the rider is on the motorcycle, his centre of mass is 1 m behind the front wheel. Find the vertical reaction forces acting through the front and rear wheels when
(i) the rider is not on the motorcycle
(ii) the rider is on the motorcycle.

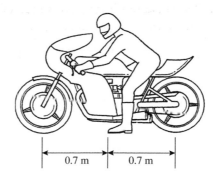

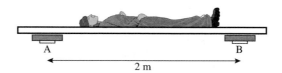

0.7 m   0.7 m

6 Karen and Jane are trying to find the positions of their centres of mass. They place a uniform board of mass 8 kg symmetrically on two bathroom scales whose centres are 2 m apart. When Karen lies flat on the board, Jane notes that scale A reads 37 kg and scale B reads 26 kg.

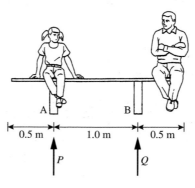

A   B

2 m

(i) Draw a diagram showing the forces acting on Karen and the board and calculate Karen's mass.

(ii) How far from the centre of scale A is her centre of mass?

7 The diagram shows two people, an adult and a child, sitting on a uniform bench of mass 40 kg; their positions are as shown. The mass of the child is 50 kg, that of the adult is 85 kg.

A   B

0.5 m   1.0 m   0.5 m

P   Q

(i) Find the reaction forces, P and Q (in N), from the ground on the two supports of the bench.

(ii) The child now moves to the mid-point of the bench. What are the new values of P and Q?

(iii) Is it possible for the child to move to a position where $P = 0$? What is the significance of a zero value for P?

(iv) What happens if the child leaves the bench?

8 The diagram shows a diving board which some children have made. It consists of a uniform plank of mass 20 kg and length 3 m, with 1 m of its length projecting out over a pool. They have put a boulder of mass 25 kg on the end over the land; and there is a support at the water's edge.

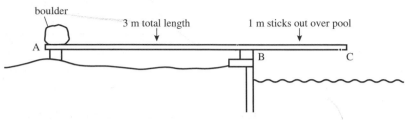

(i) Find the forces at the two supports when nobody is using the diving board.

(ii) A child of mass 50 kg is standing on the end of the diving board over the pool. What are the forces at the two supports?

(iii) Some older children arrive and take over the diving board. One of these is a heavy boy of mass 90 kg. What is the reaction at A if the board begins to tip over?

(iv) How far can the boy walk from B before the board tips over?

9 A lorry of mass 5000 kg is driven across a Bailey bridge of mass 20 tonnes. The bridge is a roadway of length 10 m which is supported at both ends.

(i) Find expressions for the reaction forces at each end of the bridge in terms of the distance x in metres travelled by the lorry from the start of the bridge.

(ii) From what point of the lorry is the distance x measured?

Two identical lorries cross the bridge at the same speed, starting at the same instant, from opposite directions.

(iii) How do the reaction forces of the supports on the bridge vary as the lorries cross the bridge?

10 A simple suspension bridge across a narrow river consists of a uniform beam, 4 m long and of mass 60 kg, supported by vertical cables attached at a distance 0.75 m from each end of the beam.

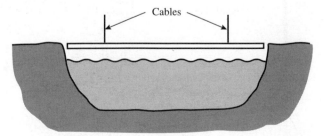

(i) Find the tension in each cable when a boy of mass 50 kg stands 1 m from the end of the bridge.

(ii) Can a couple walking hand-in-hand cross the bridge safely, without it tipping, if their combined mass is 115 kg?

(iii) What is the mass of a person standing on the end of the bridge when the tension in one cable is four times that in the other cable?

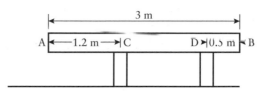

11 The diagram shows a stone slab AB of mass 1 tonne resting on two supports, C and D. The stone is uniform and has length 3 m. The supports are at distances 1.2 m and 0.5 m from the end.

(i) Find the reaction forces at the two supports.

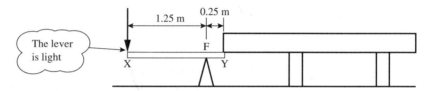

Local residents are worried that the arrangement is unsafe since their children play on the stone.

(ii) How many children each of mass 50 kg would need to stand at A in order to tip the stone over?

The stone's owner decides to move the support at C to a point nearer to A. To take the weight of the slab while doing this, he sets up the lever system shown in the diagram. The distance XF is 1.25 m and FY is 0.25 m.

(iii) What downward force applied at X would reduce the reaction force at C to zero (and so allow the support to be moved)?

12 Four seamen are using a light capstan to pull in their ship's anchor at a steady rate. One of them is shown in the diagram. The diameter of the capstan's drum is 1 m and the spokes on which the men are pushing each project 2 m from the centre of the capstan. Each man is pushing with a force of 300 N, horizontally and at right angles to his spoke. The anchor cable is taut; it passes over a frictionless pulley and then makes an angle of 20° with the horizontal.

(i) Find the tension in the cable.

The mass of the ship is 2000 tonnes.

(ii) Find the acceleration of the ship, assuming that no other horizontal forces act on the ship.

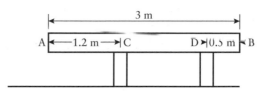

In fact the acceleration of the ship is $0.0015\,\text{ms}^{-2}$. Part of the difference can be explained by friction with the capstan, resulting in a resisting moment of $300\,\text{Nm}$, the rest by the force of resistance, $R\,\text{N}$, to the ship passing through the water.

(iii) Find the value of R.

Set up the apparatus shown in figure 3.22 below and experiment with two or more weights in different positions.

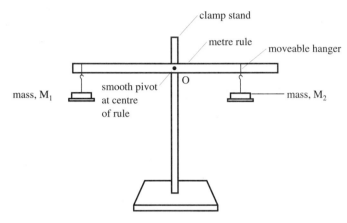

Figure 3.22

Record your results in a table showing weights, distances from O and moments about O.

Two masses are suspended from the rule in such a way that the rule balances in a horizontal position. What happens when the rule is then moved to an inclined position and released?

Now attach a pulley as in figure 3.23. Start with equal weights and measure d and l. Then try different weights and pulley positions.

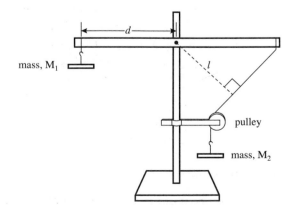

Figure 3.23

The moment of a force which acts at an angle

From the experiment you will have seen that the moment of a force about the pivot depends on the *perpendicular distance* from the pivot to the line of the force.

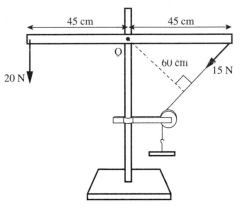

Figure 3.24

In figure 3.24, where the system remains at rest, the moment about O of the 20 N force is $20 \times 0.45 = 9$ Nm. The moment about O of the 15 N force is $-15 \times 0.6 = -9$ Nm. The system is in equilibrium even through unequal forces act at equal distances from the pivot.

The magnitude of the moment of the force F about O in figure 3.25 is given by

$$F \times l = Fd \sin \alpha$$

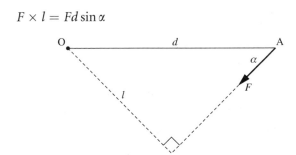

Figure 3.25

Alternatively the moment can be found by noting that the force F can be resolved into components $F \cos \alpha$ parallel to AO and $F \sin \alpha$ perpendicular to AO, both acting through A (figure 3.26). The moment of each component can be found and then summed to give the total moment.

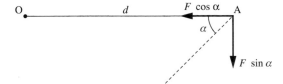

Figure 3.26

The moment of the component along AO is zero because it acts through O. The magnitude of the moment of the perpendicular component is $F \sin \alpha \times d$ so the total moment is $Fd \sin \alpha$, as expected.

EXAMPLE 3.3

A force of 40 N is exerted on a rod as shown. Find the moment of the force about the point marked O.

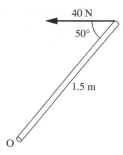

Figure 3.27

SOLUTION

In order to calculate the moment, the perpendicular distance between O and the line of action of the force must be found. This is shown on the diagram.

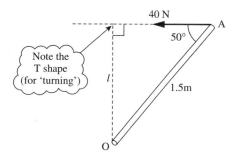

Figure 3.28

Here $l = 1.5 \times \sin 50°$.

So the moment about O is

$$F \times l = 40 \times (1.5 \times \sin 50°)$$

$$= 46.0 \text{ Nm.}$$

Alternatively you can resolve the 40 N force into components as in the next diagram.

The component of the force parallel to AO is $40 \cos 50°$ N. The component perpendicular to AO is $40 \sin 50°$ (or $40 \cos 40°$) N.

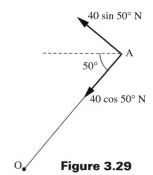

So the moment about O is
$40 \sin 50° \times 1.5 = 60 \cos 40°$
$$= 46.0 \text{ Nm as before.}$$

Figure 3.29

EXAMPLE 3.4

A sign outside a pub is attached to a light rod of length 1 m which is freely hinged to the wall and supported in a vertical plane by a light string as in the diagram. The sign is assumed to be a uniform rectangle of mass 10 kg. The angle of the string to the horizontal is 25°.

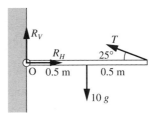

Figure 3.30

(i) Find the tension in the string.

(ii) Find the magnitude and direction of the reaction force of the hinge on the sign.

SOLUTION

(i) The diagram shows the forces acting on the rod, where R_H and R_V are the magnitudes of the horizontal and vertical components of the reaction **R** on the rod at the wall.

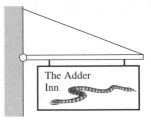

Taking moments about O

$$R \times 0 - 10g \times 0.5 + T \sin 25° \times 1 = 0$$

Figure 3.31

$$\Rightarrow T \sin 25° = 5g$$

$$T = 116$$

The tension is 116 N.

(ii) You can resolve to find the reaction at the wall.

Horizontally: $\qquad R_H = T \cos 25°$

$$\Rightarrow R_H = 105$$

Vertically: $\qquad R_V + T \sin 25° = 10g$

$$\Rightarrow R_V = 10g - 5g = 49$$

$$R = \sqrt{105^2 + 49^2}$$
$$= 116$$
$$\theta = \arctan\left(\tfrac{49}{105}\right) = 25°$$

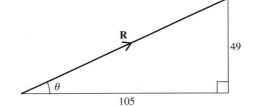

Figure 3.32

The reaction at the hinge has magnitude 116 N and acts at 25° above the horizontal.

❓ Is it by chance that R and T have the same magnitude and act at the same angle to the horizontal?

EXAMPLE 3.5

A uniform ladder is standing on rough ground and leaning against a smooth wall at an angle of 60° to the ground. The ladder has length 4 m and mass 15 kg. Find the normal reaction forces at the wall and ground and the friction force at the ground.

SOLUTION

The diagram shows the forces acting on the ladder. The forces are in newtons.

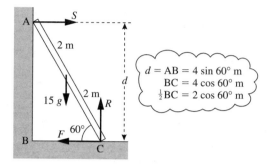

$$d = AB = 4 \sin 60° \text{ m}$$
$$BC = 4 \cos 60° \text{ m}$$
$$\tfrac{1}{2}BC = 2 \cos 60° \text{ m}$$

Figure 3.33

The diagram shows that there are three unknown forces S, R and F so we need three equations from which to find them. If the ladder remains at rest (in equilibrium) then the resultant force is zero and the resultant moment is zero. These two conditions provide the three necessary equations.

Equilibrium of horizontal components: $S - F = 0$ ①

Equilibrium of vertical components: $R - 15g = 0$ ②

Moments about the foot of the ladder:

$$R \times 0 + F \times 0 + 15g \times 2 \cos 60° - S \times 4 \sin 60° = 0$$

$$\Rightarrow \quad 147 - 4S \sin 60° = 0 \quad ③$$

$$\Rightarrow \quad S = \frac{147}{4 \sin 60°} = 42.4$$

From ① $F = S = 42.4$
From ② $R = 147.$

The force at the wall is 42.4 N, those at the ground are 42.4 N horizontally and 147 N vertically.

EXAMPLE 3.6

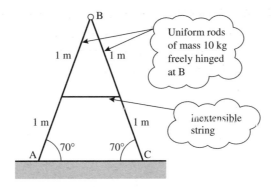

Figure 3.34

Figure 3.34 shows a model for a step-ladder standing on a smooth horizontal floor.

(i) Draw a diagram to show the forces acting on both rods AB and BC.

(ii) Explain why the internal forces in the hinge at B are horizontal.

(iii) Calculate the tension in the string.

A woman of mass 56 kg stands on a step 0.5 m from A. Calculate

(iv) the new reaction at C

(v) the tension in the string and the magnitude of the reaction at B.

SOLUTION

(i) Figure 3.35 shows the forces acting when the ground is smooth.

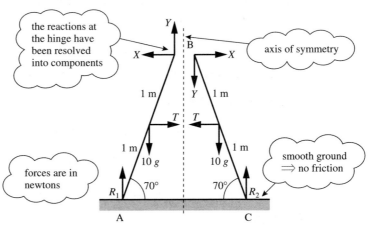

Figure 3.35

(ii) By Newton's third law, the reactions at B are equal and opposite. Also by the symmetry of the step-ladder and the forces, the vertical components are equal in magnitude and direction. Both conditions can be satisfied only if $Y = 0$ and $R_1 = R_2$.

(iii) The two parts of the ladder can be treated separately.

Resolving horizontally for AB or BC $\Rightarrow X = T$

Taking moments about C for BC
$$\Rightarrow 10g \times 1 \cos 70° + T \times 1 \sin 70° = X \times 2 \sin 70°$$

Substituting for X $\quad\quad\quad\quad 10g\cos 70° = 2T\sin 70° - T\sin 70°$

$$\Rightarrow T = \frac{10g\cos 70°}{\sin 70°}$$

The tension in the string is 35.7 N.

(iv) When a woman stands on a step, the forces are no longer symmetrical so

$$Y \neq 0 \text{ and } R_1 \neq R_2$$

There are now several possible ways forward. You can treat the ladder as a whole or each part separately but it is best to try to avoid writing down too many equations involving a lot of unknowns.

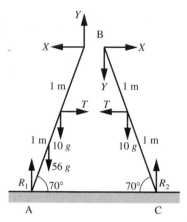

Figure 3.36

Take moments about A for the whole system:

$$R_2 \times 4\cos 70° = 10g \times 3\cos 70° + 10g \times 1\cos 70° + 56g \times 0.5\cos 70°$$
$$\Rightarrow \quad\quad 4R_2 = 30g + 10g + 28g$$
$$R_2 = 17g$$

Divide by $\cos 70°$ ①

The new reaction at C is 167 N.

(v) Take moments about B for BC:

$$R_2 \times 2\cos 70° = 10g \times 1\cos 70° + T \times 1\sin 70°$$

Substituting from ① $\quad \Rightarrow (34g - 10g)\cos 70° = T\sin 70°$

$$\Rightarrow \quad\quad\quad\quad\quad T = \frac{24g\cos 70°}{\sin 70°}$$

The tension in the string is 85.6 N.

Resolve vertically for BC: $\quad R_2 = 10g + Y$

$$\Rightarrow Y = 7g = 68.6$$

horizontally: $\quad\quad\quad X = T = 85.6$

The reaction at B has magnitude $\sqrt{(85.6^2 + 68.6^2)} = 110$ N

 Notice that the extra vertical force due to the woman's weight has an effect on all the forces including those that are horizontal. You cannot assume that any of the reactions remain as they were.

? Suggest an alternative method for part (iii) and check that it gives the same answer.

1 Find the moment about O of each of the forces illustrated below.

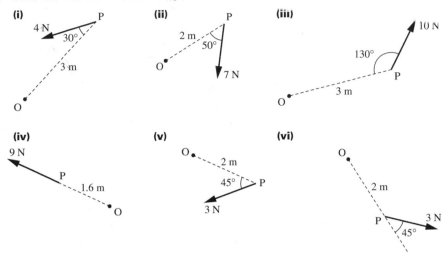

(i)

(ii)

(iii)

(iv)

(v)

(vi)

2 The diagram shows three children pushing a playground roundabout. Hannah and David want it to go one way but Rabina wants it to go the other way. Who wins?

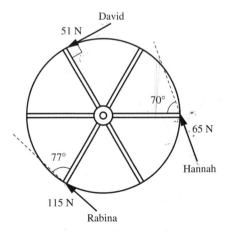

3 The operating instructions for a small crane specify that when the jib is at an angle of 25° above the horizontal, the maximum safe load for the crane is 5000 kg. Assuming that this maximum load is determined by the maximum moment that the pivot can support, what is the maximum safe load when the angle between the jib and the horizontal is:

(i) 40°   **(ii)** an angle θ?

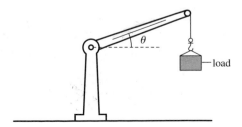

4 In each of these diagrams, a uniform beam of mass 5 kg and length 4 m, freely hinged at one end, A, is in equilibrium. Find the magnitude of the force T in each case.

(i)

(ii)

(iii)

A

30°

2 m

30°

T

5g N

1 m

1 m

T

A

30°

5g N

10 N

T

50°

2 m

A

20°

5g N

5 The diagram shows a uniform rectangular sign ABCD, 3 m × 2 m, of weight 20 N. It is freely hinged at A and supported by the string CE, which makes an angle of 30° with the horizontal. The tension in the string is T (in N).

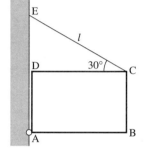

  (i) Resolve the tension T into horizontal and vertical components.

  (ii) Hence show that the moment of the tension in the string about A is given by

$$2T\cos 30° + 3T\sin 30°.$$

  (iii) Write down the moment of the sign's weight about A.

  (iv) Hence show that $T = 9.28$.

  (v) Hence find the horizontal and vertical components of the reaction on the sign at the hinge, A.

You can also find the moment of the tension in the string about A as $d \times T$, where d is the length of AF as shown in the diagram.

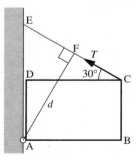

  (vi) Find (a) the angle ACD (b) the length d.

  (vii) Show that you get the same value for T when it is calculated in this way.

6 The diagram shows a simple crane. The weight of the jib (AB) may be ignored. The crane is in equilibrium in the position shown.

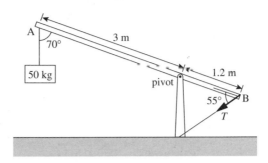

(i) By taking moments about the pivot, find the magnitude of the tension T (in N).

(ii) Find the reaction of the pivot on the jib in the form of components parallel and perpendicular to the jib.

(iii) Show that the total moment about the end A of the forces acting on the jib is zero.

(iv) What would happen if
  (a) the rope holding the 50 kg mass snapped
  (b) the rope with tension T snapped?

7 A uniform plank, AB, of mass 50 kg and length 6 m is in equilibrium leaning against a smooth wall at an angle of 60° to the horizontal. The lower end, A, is on rough horizontal ground.

(i) Draw a diagram showing all the forces acting on the plank.

(ii) Write down the total moment about A of all the forces acting on the plank.

(iii) Find the normal reaction of the wall on the plank at point B.

(iv) Find the frictional force on the foot of the plank. What can you deduce about the coefficient of friction between the ground and the plank?

(v) Show that the total moment about B of all the forces acting on the plank is zero.

8 A uniform ladder of mass 20 kg and length $2l$ rests in equilibrium with its upper end against a smooth vertical wall and its lower end on a rough horizontal floor. The coefficient of friction between the ladder and the floor is μ. The normal reaction at the wall is S, the frictional force at the ground is F and the normal reaction at the ground is R. The ladder makes an angle α with the horizontal.

(i) Draw a diagram showing the forces acting on the ladder.

For each of the cases, (a) $\alpha = 60°$, (b) $\alpha = 45°$

(ii) find the magnitudes of S, F and R

(iii) find the least possible value of μ.

9 The diagram shows a car's hand brake. The force F is exerted by the hand in operating the brake, and this creates a tension T in the brake cable. The hand brake is freely pivoted at point B and is assumed to be light.

(i) Draw a diagram showing all the forces acting on the hand brake.

(ii) What is the required magnitude of force F if the tension in the brake cable is to be 1000 N?

(iii) A child applies the hand brake with a force of 10 N. What is the tension in the brake cable?

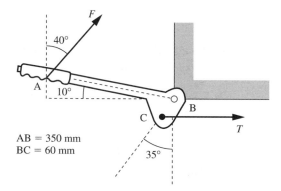

AB = 350 mm
BC = 60 mm

10 The diagram shows four tugs manoeuvring a ship. A and C are pushing it, B and D are pulling it.

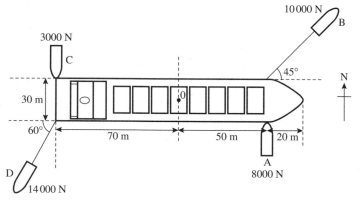

(i) Show that the resultant force on the ship is less than 100 N.

(ii) Find the overall turning moment on the ship about its centre point, O.

A breeze starts to blow from the South, causing a total force of 2000 N to act uniformly along the length of the ship, at right angles to it.

(iii) How (assuming B and D continue to apply the same forces) can tugs A and C counteract the sideways force on the ship by altering the forces with which they are pushing, while maintaining the same overall moment about the centre of the ship?

11 Two equal, uniform rods, AB and BC, of weight W are freely jointed at B and rest symmetrically with ends A and C in contact with a rough horizontal surface, as shown in the diagram.

(i) Explain why the force on each rod at B is horizontal.

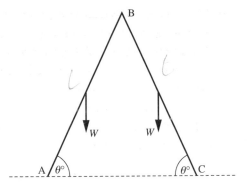

(ii) Draw a diagram showing the horizontal and vertical components of the forces acting on the rod AB.

Each rod is inclined at θ to the horizontal and is about to slip.

(iii) Write down equations for the horizontal and vertical equilibrium of rod AB and show that the frictional force at A is μW, where μ is the coefficient of friction between the rod and the surface at A.

(iv) Take moments about A. Hence show that $\tan\theta = \frac{1}{2}\mu$

(v) Interpret the equation $\tan\theta = \frac{1}{2}\mu$ as $\mu \to 0$ in terms of the equilibrium of the rods.

[MEI]

12 The boom of a fishing boat may be used as a simple crane. The boom AB is uniform, 8 m long and has a mass of 30 kg. It is freely hinged at the end A.

In figure (A), the boom shown is in equilibrium supported at C by the boat's rail, where the length AC is 3.5 m. The boom is horizontal and has a load of mass 20 kg suspended from the end B.

(i) Draw a diagram showing all the forces acting on the boom AB.

(ii) Find the force exerted on the boom by the rail at C.

(iii) Calculate the magnitude and direction of the force acting on the boom at A.

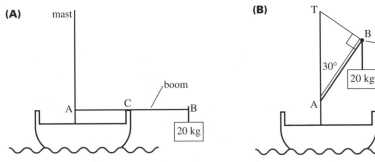

It is more usual to use the boom in a position such as the one shown in figure (B). AT is vertical and the boom is held in equilibrium by the rope section TB, which is perpendicular to it. Angle TAB = 30°. A load of mass 20 kg is supported by a rope passing over a small, smooth pulley at B. The rope then runs parallel to the boom to a fixing point at A.

(iv) Find the tension in the rope section TB when the load is stationary.

[MEI, part]

13 (i) Draw a diagram showing the forces acting on an inclined ladder which is standing on a horizontal floor and leaning against a vertical wall. Explain why the ladder cannot be in equilibrium if the floor is frictionless, even if the wall is rough.

(ii) A uniform ladder of length 8 m and mass 20 kg is inclined at 60° to the horizontal against a smooth vertical wall. A 60 kg man is standing on the ladder x m from its lower end. The horizontal floor has coefficient of friction 0.4 with the base of the ladder. The ladder is about to slip.
   (a) Show that the frictional force on the ladder is $32g$ N.
   (b) Find the reaction of the wall on the ladder.
   (c) Show that x is about 6.06 m.

[MEI]

14 Jules is cleaning windows. Her ladder is uniform and stands on rough ground at an angle of 60° to the horizontal and with the top end resting on the edge of a smooth window sill. The ladder has mass 12 kg and length 2.8 m and Jules has mass 56 kg.
   (i) Draw a diagram to show the forces on the ladder when nobody is standing on it. Show that the reaction at the sill is then $3g$ N.
   (ii) Find the friction and normal reaction forces at the foot of the ladder.

Jules needs to be sure that the ladder will not slip however high she climbs.
   (iii) Find the least possible value of μ for the ladder to be safe at 60° to the horizontal.
   (iv) The value of μ is in fact 0.4. How far up the ladder can Jules stand before it begins to slip?

15 The diagram shows a uniform girder AB of weight 3000 N and length 6 m which has been hoisted into the air by a crane. The lengths of the ropes AC and BC are both 5 m. The tension in AC is T_1 N, that in BC is T_2 N. The girder makes an angle α with the horizontal. The point X is directly below C and M is the mid-point of AB.

Fred, whose weight is 1000 N, was sitting on the girder when it was hoisted and now finds himself in mid-air. At the time of the question the girder and Fred are stationary. Fred is at point F where AF = 4 m and BF = 2 m.

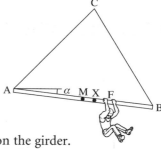

   (i) Draw a diagram showing the forces acting on the girder.
   (ii) By taking moments about C find the distances MX and FX. Calculate the length CM and hence find α.
   (iii) Find the values T_1 and T_2.
   (iv) Fred decides to try to reach the point B. What is the value of α when he gets there?

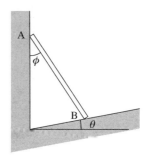

16 The diagram shows a uniform ladder AB of mass m and length $2l$ resting in equilibrium with its upper end A against a smooth vertical wall and its lower end B on a smooth inclined plane. The inclined plane makes an angle θ with the horizontal and the ladder makes an angle ϕ with the wall.

(i) Find the value of ϕ when θ equals 10°.

(ii) What is the relationship between ϕ and θ?

Sliding and toppling

The photograph shows a double decker bus on a test ramp. The angle of the ramp to the horizontal is slowly increased.

❓ What happens to the bus? Would a loaded bus behave differently from the empty bus in the photograph?

EXPERIMENT

The diagrams show a force being applied in different positions to a cereal packet.

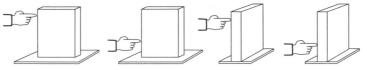

Figure 3.37

In which case do you think the packet is most likely to fall over? In which case is it most likely to slide? Investigate your answers practically, using boxes of different shapes.

? Figure 3.38 shows the cereal packet placed on a slope. Is the box more likely to topple or slide as the angle of the slope to the horizontal increases?

To what extent is this situation comparable to that of the bus on the test ramp?

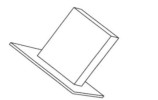

Figure 3.38

Two critical cases

When an object stands on a surface, the only forces acting are its weight W and the *resultant* of all the contact forces between the surfaces which must act through a point on both surfaces. This resultant contact force is often resolved into two components: the friction, F, parallel to any possible sliding and the normal reaction, R, perpendicular to F as in figures 3.39–3.41.

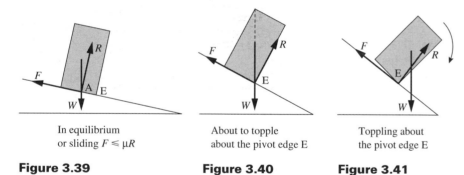

In equilibrium or sliding $F \leqslant \mu R$	About to topple about the pivot edge E	Toppling about the pivot edge E
Figure 3.39	**Figure 3.40**	**Figure 3.41**

Equilibrium can be broken in two ways:

(i) *The object is on the point of sliding*, then $F = \mu R$ according to our model.

(ii) *The object is on the point of toppling*. The pivot is at the lowest point of contact which is the point E in figure 3.40. In this critical case:

- the centre of mass is directly above E so the weight acts vertically downwards through E;
- the resultant reaction of the plane on the object acts through E, vertically upwards. This is the resultant of F and R.

? Why does the object topple in figure 3.41?

When three non-parallel forces are in equilibrium, their lines of action must be concurrent (they must all pass through one point). Otherwise there is a resultant moment about the point where two of them meet as in figure 3.41.

EXAMPLE 3.7

An increasing force P N is applied to a block, as shown in figure 3.42, until the block moves. The coefficient of friction between the block and the plane is 0.4. Does it slide or topple?

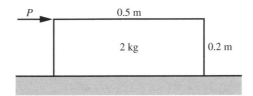

Figure 3.42

SOLUTION

The forces acting are shown in figure 3.43. The normal reaction may be thought of as a single force acting somewhere within the area of contact. When toppling occurs (or is about to occur) the line of action is through the edge about which it topples.

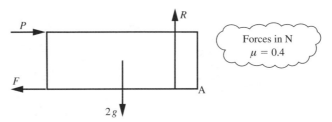

Figure 3.43

Until the block moves, it is in equilibrium.

Horizontally $\qquad$ $P = F$ $\qquad\qquad$ ①

Vertically $\qquad$ $R = 2g$ $\qquad\qquad$ ②

If *sliding* is about to occur $\qquad$ $F = \mu R$

From ① $\qquad$ $P = \mu R = 0.4 \times 2g$

$\qquad\qquad\qquad\qquad = 7.84$

If the block is about to *topple*, then A is the pivot point and the reaction of the plane on the block acts at A. Taking moments about A gives

$(\curvearrowleft)$ $\qquad\qquad$ $2g \times 0.25 - P \times 0.2 = 0$

$\qquad\qquad\qquad\qquad$ $P = 24.5$ $\qquad$ *R acts through A*

So to slide P needs to exceed 7.84 N but to topple it needs to exceed 24.5 N: the block will slide before it topples.

EXAMPLE 3.8

A rectangular block of mass 3 kg is placed on a slope as shown below. The angle α is gradually increased. What happens to the block, given that the coefficient of friction between the block and slope is 0.6?

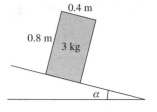

SOLUTION

Figure 3.44

Check for possible sliding

Figure 3.45 shows the forces acting when the block is in equilibrium.

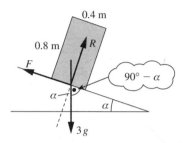

Figure 3.45

Resolve parallel to the slope: $F = 3g \sin \alpha$
Perpendicular to the slope: $R = 3g \cos \alpha$

When the block is on the point of sliding $F = \mu R$ so

$$3g \sin \alpha = \mu \times 3g \cos \alpha$$
$$\Rightarrow \quad \tan \alpha = \mu = 0.6$$
$$\Rightarrow \quad \alpha = 31°$$

The block is on the point of sliding when $\alpha = 31°$.

Check for possible toppling

When the block is on the point of toppling about the edge E the centre of mass is vertically above E, as shown in figure 3.46.

Then the angle α is given by:

$$\tan \alpha = \frac{0.4}{0.8}$$
$$\alpha = 26.6°$$

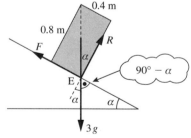

Figure 3.46

The block topples when $\alpha = 26.6°$.

The angle for sliding $(31°)$ is greater than the angle for toppling $(26.6°)$, so the block topples without sliding when $\alpha = 26.6°$.

❓ Is it possible for sliding and toppling to occur for the same angle?

1 A force of magnitude P N acts as shown on a block resting on a horizontal plane. The coefficient of friction between the block and the plane is 0.7.

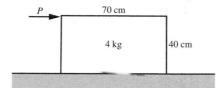

The magnitude of the force P is gradually increased from zero.
(i) Find the magnitude of P if the block is on the point of sliding assuming it does not topple.
(ii) Find the magnitude of P if the block is on the point of toppling assuming it does not slide.
(iii) Does the block slide or topple?

2 A solid uniform cuboid is placed on a horizontal surface. A force P is applied as shown in the diagram.
(i) If the block is on the point of sliding express P in terms of μ, the coefficient of friction between the block and the plane.

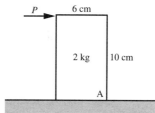

(ii) Find the magnitude of P if the cuboid is on the point of toppling.
(iii) For what values of μ will the block slide before it topples?
(iv) For what values of μ will the block topple before it slides?

3 A horizontal force of increasing magnitude is applied to the middle of the face of a 50 cm uniform cube, at right angles to the face. The coefficient of friction between the cube and the surface is 0.4 and the cube is on a level surface. What happens to the cube?

4 A solid uniform cube of side 4 cm and weight 60 N is situated on a rough horizontal plane. The coefficient of friction between the cube and the plane is 0.4. A force P N acts in the middle of one of the edges of the top of the cube, as shown in the diagram.

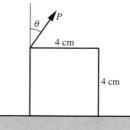

In the cases when the value of θ is **(a)** 60° **(b)** 80°, find
(i) the force P needed to make the cube slide, assuming it does not topple
(ii) the force P needed to make the cube topple, assuming it does not slide
(iii) whether it first slides or topples as the force P is increased.

For what value of θ does toppling and sliding occur for the same value of P, and what is that value of P?

5 A uniform rectangular block of height 30 cm and width 10 cm is placed on a rough plane inclined at an angle α to the horizontal. The block lies on the plane with its length horizontal. The coefficient of friction between the block and the plane is 0.25.

(i) Assuming that it does not topple, for what value of α does the block just slide?

(ii) Assuming that it does not slide, for what value of α does the block just topple?

(iii) The angle α is increased slowly from an initial value of $0°$. Which happens first, sliding or toppling?

6 A solid uniform cuboid, 10 cm × 20 cm × 50 cm, is to stand on an inclined plane, which makes an angle α with the horizontal. One edge of the cuboid is to be parallel to the line of the slope. The coefficient of friction between the cuboid and the plane is μ.

(i) Which face of the cuboid should be placed on the slope to make it

   (a) least likely and   (b) most likely to topple?

(ii) How does the cuboid's orientation influence the likelihood of it sliding?

(iii) Find the range of values of μ in the situations where

   (a) it will slide first whatever its orientation

   (b) it will topple first whatever its orientation.

7 A cube of side 4 cm and mass 100 g is acted on by a force as shown in the diagram.

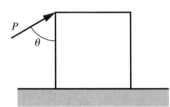

The coefficient of friction between the cube and the plane is 0.3. What happens to the cube if

(i) $\theta = 45°$ and $P = 0.3$ N

(ii) $\theta = 15°$ and $P = 0.45$ N?

8

A man is trying to move a uniform scaffold plank of length 3 m and weight 150 N which is resting on horizontal ground. You may assume that he exerts a slowly increasing force of magnitude P N at a constant angle θ to the vertical and at right angles to the edge CD, as shown in the diagram above. As P increases, the plank will either slide or start to turn about the end AB depending on the values of θ and the coefficient of friction μ between the plank and the ground.

Assume that the plank slides before it turns and is on the point of sliding.

(i) Show that the normal reaction of the ground on the plank is $(150 - P\cos\theta)\,\text{N}$.

(ii) Obtain two expressions involving the frictional force acting on the plank and deduce that

$$P = \frac{150\mu}{\sin\theta + \mu\cos\theta}$$

Assume now that the plank starts to turn about the edge AB before it slides and is on the point of turning.

(iii) Where is the line of action of the normal reaction of the ground on the plank?

(iv) Show that $P = \dfrac{75}{\cos\theta}$

Given that the plank slides before it turns about AB as the force P is gradually increased,

(v) find the relationship between μ and θ. Simplify your answer.

[MEI]

INVESTIGATIONS

1 Finding your centre of mass

How could you use two bathroom scales and a narrow board to find your centre of mass when your body is in various positions? (See exercise 3A question 6.) It is recommended that heavy weights such as books are carried on a bicycle in panniers rather than a rucksack. Use a similar method to estimate the difference in the height of your centre of mass when carrying books and kit etc. in these two positions.

2 Baby buggy

Borrow a baby buggy and investigate its stability. How stable is it when you hang some shopping on its handle?

How could the design of the buggy be altered to improve its stability?

Think about the handling of the buggy in other situations. Would your changes cause any problems?

3 **Toolbox**

Which tools in a typical tool box or kitchen drawer depend upon moments for their successful operation?

4 **Sliding and toppling**

Make a pile of rough bricks on a board, then raise one edge of the board so that it slopes. Investigate what happens as the angle of the slope is increased.

KEY POINTS

1 The moment of a force F about a point O is given by the product Fd where d is the perpendicular distance from O to the line of action of the force.

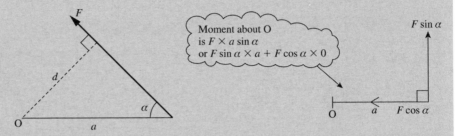

Moment about O is $F \times a \sin \alpha$ or $F \sin \alpha \times a + F \cos \alpha \times 0$

2 The S.I. unit for moment is the newton metre (Nm).

3 Anticlockwise moments are usually called positive, clockwise negative.

4 If a body is in equilibrium the sum of the moments of the forces acting on it, about any point, is zero.

5 When three non-parallel forces are in equilibrium, their lines of action are concurrent.

6 Two parallel forces P and Q $(P > Q)$ are equivalent to a single force $P + Q$ when P and Q are in the same direction and $P - Q$ when they are in opposite directions. The line of action of the equivalent force is found by taking moments.

Centre of mass

Let man then contemplate the whole of nature in her full and grand mystery ... It is an infinite sphere, the centre of which is everywhere, the circumference nowhere.

Blaise Pascal

❓ Figure 4.1, which is drawn to scale, shows a mobile suspended from the point P. The horizontal rods and the strings are light but the geometrically shaped pieces are made of uniform heavy card. Does the mobile balance? If it does, what can you say about the position of its centre of mass?

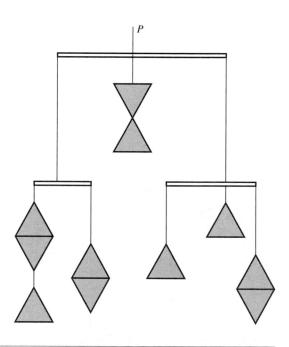

Figure 4.1

❓ Where is the centre of mass of the gymnast in the picture (right)?

You have met the concept of centre of mass in the context of two general models.

- *The particle model*
  The centre of mass is the single point at which the whole mass of the body may be taken to be situated.
- *The rigid body model*
  The centre of mass is the balance point of a body with size and shape.

The following examples show how to calculate the position of the centre of mass of a body.

EXAMPLE 4.1

An object consists of **three** point masses 8 kg, 5 kg and 4 kg attached to a rigid light rod as shown.

O

Figure 4.2

Calculate the distance of the centre of mass of the object from end O. (Ignore the mass of the rod.)

SOLUTION

Suppose the centre of mass C is $\bar{x}$ m from O. If a pivot were at this position the rod would balance.

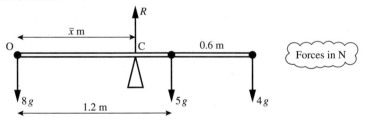

Figure 4.3

For equilibrium $\qquad R = 8g + 5g + 4g = 17g$

Taking moments of the forces about O gives:

Total clockwise moment $\qquad = (8g \times 0) + (5g \times 1.2) + (4g \times 1.8)$
$\qquad\qquad\qquad\qquad\qquad = 13.2g \, \text{Nm}$

Total anticlockwise moment $= R\bar{x}$
$\qquad\qquad\qquad\qquad\qquad = 17g\bar{x} \, \text{Nm}.$

The overall moment must be zero for the rod to be in balance, so

$$17g\bar{x} - 13.2g = 0$$
$$\Rightarrow \qquad\qquad 17\bar{x} = 13.2$$
$$\Rightarrow \qquad\qquad \bar{x} = \frac{13.2}{17} = 0.776.$$

The centre of mass is 0.776 m from the end O of the rod.

Note that although g was included in the calculation, it cancelled out. The answer depends only on the masses and their distances from the origin and not on the value of g. This leads to the following definition for the position of the centre of mass.

Definition

Consider a set of n point masses $m_1, m_2, \ldots, m_n$ attached to a rigid light rod (whose mass is neglected) at positions $x_1, x_2, \ldots, x_n$ from one end O. The situation is shown in figure 4.4.

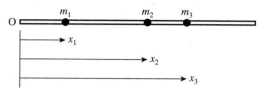

Figure 4.4

The position, $\bar{x}$, of the centre of mass relative to O, is defined by the equation:

moment of whole mass at centre of mass = sum of moments of individual masses
$$(m_1 + m_2 + m_3 + \ldots)\bar{x} = m_1 x_1 + m_2 x_2 + m_3 x_3 + \ldots$$

or

$$M\bar{x} = \sum_{i=1}^{n} m_i x_i$$

where M is the total mass (or Σm_i).

EXAMPLE 4.2

A uniform rod of length 2 m has mass 5 kg. Masses of 4 kg and 6 kg are fixed at each end of the rod. Find the centre of mass of the rod.

SOLUTION

Since the rod is uniform, it can be treated as a point mass at its centre. Figure 4.5 illustrates this situation.

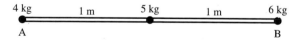

Figure 4.5

Taking the end A as origin,

$$M\bar{x} = \Sigma m_i x_i$$
$$(4 + 5 + 6)\bar{x} = 4 \times 0 + 5 \times 1 + 6 \times 2$$
$$15\bar{x} = 17$$
$$\bar{x} = \tfrac{17}{15}$$
$$= 1\tfrac{2}{15}$$

So the centre of mass is 1.133 m from the 4 kg point mass.

Check that the rod would balance about a pivot $1\tfrac{2}{15}$ m from A.

A rod AB of mass 1.1 kg and length 1.2 m has its centre of mass 0.48 m from the end A. What mass should be attached to the end B to ensure that the centre of mass is at the mid-point of the rod?

SOLUTION

Let the extra mass be m kg.

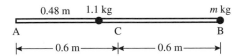

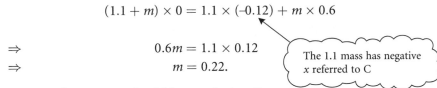

Figure 4.6

Method 1 Refer to the mid-point, C, as origin, so $\bar{x} = 0$. Then

$$(1.1 + m) \times 0 = 1.1 \times (-0.12) + m \times 0.6$$

$\Rightarrow \qquad\qquad 0.6m = 1.1 \times 0.12$

$\Rightarrow \qquad\qquad m = 0.22.$

> The 1.1 mass has negative x referred to C

A mass of 220 grams should be attached to B.

Method 2 Refer to the end A, as origin, so $\bar{x} = 0.6$. Then

$$(1.1 + m) \times 0.6 = 1.1 \times 0.48 + m \times 1.2$$

$\Rightarrow \qquad 0.66 + 0.6m = 0.528 + 1.2m$

$\Rightarrow \qquad\qquad 0.132 = 0.6m$

$\qquad\qquad\qquad m = 0.22$ as before.

Composite bodies

The position of the centre of mass of a composite body such as a cricket bat, tennis racquet or golf club is important to sports people who like to feel its balance. If the body is symmetric then the centre of mass will lie on the axis of symmetry. The next example shows how to model a composite body as a system of point masses so that the methods of the previous section can be used to find the centre of mass.

A squash racquet of mass 200 g and total length 70 cm consists of a handle of mass 150 g whose centre of mass is 20 cm from the end, and a frame of mass 50 g, whose centre of mass is 55 cm from the end.

Find the distance of the centre of mass from the end of the handle.

SOLUTION

Figure 4.7 shows the squash racquet and its dimensions.

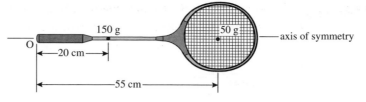

Figure 4.7

The centre of mass lies on
the axis of symmetry. Model
the handle as a point mass
of 0.15 kg a distance 0.2 m
from O and the frame as a
point mass of 0.05 kg a
distance 0.55 m from the end O.

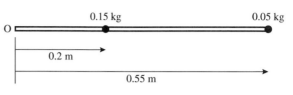

Figure 4.8

The distance, $\bar{x}$, of the centre of mass from O is given by

$$(0.15 + 0.05)\,\bar{x} = (0.15 \times 0.2) + (0.05 \times 0.55)$$
$$\bar{x} = 0.2875.$$

The centre of mass of the squash racquet is 28.75 cm from the end of the handle.

Centres of mass for different shapes

If an object has an axis of symmetry, like the squash racquet in the example above, then the centre of mass lies on it.

The table below gives the position of the centre of mass of some uniform objects that you may encounter, or wish to include within models of composite bodies.

Body	Position of centre of mass	Diagram
Solid cone or pyramid	$\dfrac{1}{4}h$ from base	
Hollow cone or pyramid	$\dfrac{1}{3}h$ from base	
Solid hemisphere	$\dfrac{3}{8}r$ from base	
Hollow hemisphere	$\dfrac{1}{2}r$ from base	
Semi-circular lamina	$\dfrac{4r}{3\pi}$ from base	

1 The diagrams show point masses attached to rigid light rods. In each case calculate the position of the centre of mass relative to the point O.

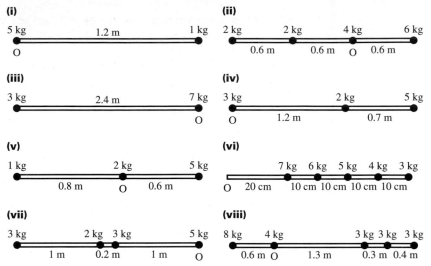

(i)

5 kg 1.2 m 1 kg
O

(ii)

2 kg 2 kg 4 kg 6 kg
0.6 m 0.6 m O 0.6 m

(iii)

3 kg 2.4 m 7 kg
O

(iv)

3 kg 2 kg 5 kg
O 1.2 m 0.7 m

(v)

1 kg 2 kg 5 kg
0.8 m O 0.6 m

(vi)

7 kg 6 kg 5 kg 4 kg 3 kg
O 20 cm 10 cm 10 cm 10 cm 10 cm

(vii)

3 kg 2 kg 3 kg 5 kg
1 m 0.2 m 1 m O

(viii)

8 kg 4 kg 3 kg 3 kg 3 kg
0.6 m O 1.3 m 0.3 m 0.4 m

2 A seesaw consists of a uniform plank 4 m long of mass 10 kg. Calculate the centre of mass when two children, of masses 20 kg and 25 kg, sit, one on each end.

3 A weightlifter's bar in a competition has mass 10 kg and length 1 m. By mistake, 50 kg is placed on one end and 60 kg on the other end. How far is the centre of mass of the bar from the centre of the bar itself?

4 The masses of the earth and the moon are 5.98×10^{24} kg and 7.38×10^{22} kg, and the distance between their centres is 3.84×10^{5} km. How far from the centre of the earth is the centre of mass of the earth–moon system?

5 A lollipop lady carries a sign which consists of a uniform rod of length 1.5 m, and mass 1 kg, on top of which is a circular disc of radius 0.25 m and mass 0.2 kg. Find the distance of the centre of mass from the free end of the stick.

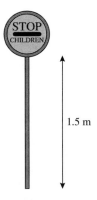

1.5 m

6 A rod has length 2 m and mass 3 kg. The centre of mass should be in the middle but due to a fault in the manufacturing process it is not. This error is corrected by placing a 200 g mass 5 cm from the centre of the rod. Where is the centre of mass of the rod itself?

7 A child's toy consists of four uniform discs, all made out of the same material. They each have thickness 2 cm and their radii are 6 cm, 5 cm, 4 cm and 3 cm. They are placed symmetrically on top of each other to form a tower. How high is the centre of mass of the tower?

8 A standard lamp consists of a uniform heavy metal base of thickness 4 cm, attached to which is a uniform metal rod of length 1.75 m and mass 0.25 kg.

What is the minimum mass for the base if the centre of mass of the lamp is no more than 12 cm from the ground?

9 A uniform scaffold pole of length 5 m has brackets bolted to it as shown in the diagram below. The mass of each bracket is 1 kg.

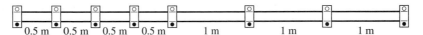

0.5 m   0.5 m   0.5 m   0.5 m   1 m   1 m   1 m

The centre of mass is 2.44 m from the left-hand end. What is the mass of the pole?

10 An object of mass m_1 is placed at one end of a light rod of length l. An object of mass m_2 is placed at the other end. Find the position of the centre of mass.

11 The diagram illustrates a mobile tower crane. It consists of the main vertical section (mass M tonnes), housing the engine, winding gear and controls, and the boom. The centre of mass of the main section is on its centre line. The boom, which has negligible mass, supports the load (L tonnes) and the counterweight (C tonnes). The main section stands on supports at P and Q, distance $2d$ m apart. The counterweight is held at a fixed distance a m from the centre line of the main section and the load at a variable distance l m.

(i) In the case when $C = 3$, $M = 10$, $L = 7$, $a = 8$, $d = 2$ and $l = 13$, find the horizontal position of the centre of mass and say what happens to the crane.

(ii) Show that for these values of C, M, a, d and l the crane will not fall over when it has no load, and find the maximum safe load that it can carry.

(iii) Formulate two inequalities in terms of C, M, L, a, d and l that must hold if the crane is to be safe loaded or unloaded.

(iv) Find, in terms of M, a, d and l, the maximum load that the crane can carry.

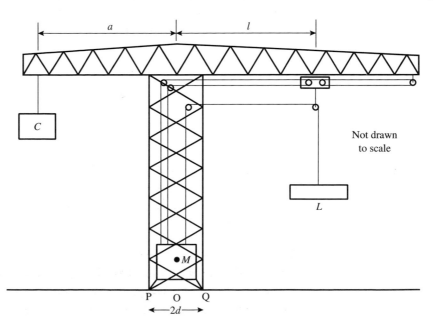

Not drawn to scale

Centre of mass for two- and three-dimensional bodies

The techniques developed for finding the centre of mass using moments can be extended into two and three dimensions.

If a two-dimensional body consists of a set of n point masses $m_1, m_2, \ldots, m_n$ located at positions $(x_1, y_1), (x_2, y_2), \ldots, (x_n, y_n)$ as in figure 4.9 then the position of the centre of mass of the body $(\bar{x}, \bar{y})$ is given by

$$M\bar{x} = \Sigma m_i x_i \text{ and } M\bar{y} = \Sigma m_i y_i$$

where $M(=\Sigma m_i)$ is the total mass of the body.

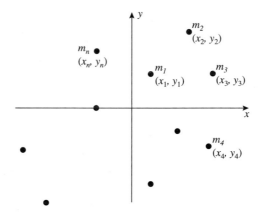

Figure 4.9

In three dimensions, the z co-ordinates are also included, to find $\bar{z}$ use

$$M\bar{z} = \Sigma m_i z_i$$

The centre of mass of any composite body in two or three dimensions can be found by replacing each component by a point mass at its centre of mass.

EXAMPLE 4.5

Joanna makes herself a pendant in the shape of a letter J made up of rectangular shapes as shown in figure 4.10.

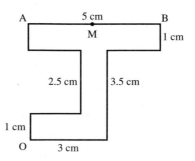

Figure 4.10

(i) Find the position of the centre of mass of the pendant.

(ii) Find the angle that AB makes with the horizontal if she hangs the pendant from a point, M, in the middle of AB.

She wishes to hang the pendant so that AB is horizontal.

(iii) How far along AB should she place the ring that the suspending chain will pass through?

SOLUTION

(i) The first step is to split the pendant into three rectangles. The centre of mass of each of these is at its middle, as shown in figure 4.11.

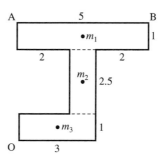

Figure 4.11

You can model the pendant as three point masses m_1, m_2 and m_3, which are proportional to the areas of the rectangular shapes. Since the areas are $5\,\text{cm}^2$, $2.5\,\text{cm}^2$ and $3\,\text{cm}^2$, the masses, in suitable units, are 5, 2.5 and 3, and the total mass is $5 + 2.5 + 3 = 10.5$ (in the same units).

The table below gives the mass and position of m_1, m_2 and m_3.

Mass		m_1	m_2	m_3	M
Mass units		5	2.5	3	10.5
Position of	x	2.5	2.5	1.5	$\bar{x}$
centre of mass	y	4	2.25	0.5	$\bar{y}$

Now it is possible to find $\bar{x}$:

$$M\bar{x} = \Sigma m_i\,x_i$$
$$10.5\bar{x} = 5 \times 2.5 + 2.5 \times 2.5 + 3 \times 1.5$$
$$\bar{x} = \frac{23.25}{10.5} = 2.2\,\text{cm}$$

Similarly for $\bar{y}$:

$$M\bar{y} = \Sigma m_i\,y_i$$
$$10.5\bar{y} = 5 \times 4 + 2.5 \times 2.25 + 3 \times 0.5$$
$$\bar{y} = \frac{27.125}{10.5} = 2.6\,\text{cm}$$

The centre of mass is at (2.2, 2.6).

(ii) When the pendant is suspended from M, the centre of mass, G, is vertically below M, as shown in figure 4.12.

The pendant hangs like the first diagram but you might find it easier to draw your own diagram like the second.

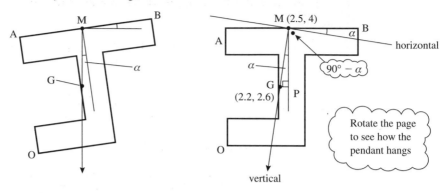

Figure 4.12

$$GP = 2.5 - 2.2 = 0.3$$
$$MP = 4.5 - 2.6 = 1.9$$
$$\therefore \qquad \tan \alpha = \frac{0.3}{1.9} \Rightarrow \alpha = 9°$$

AB makes an angle of 9° with the horizontal (or 8.5° working with unrounded figures).

(iii) For AB to be horizontal the point of suspension must be directly above the centre of mass, and so it is 2.2 cm from A.

EXAMPLE 4.6

Find the centre of mass of a body consisting of a square plate of mass 3 kg and side length 2 m, with small objects of mass 1 kg, 2 kg, 4 kg and 5 kg at the corners of the square.

SOLUTION

Figure 4.13 shows the square plate, with the origin taken at the corner at which the 1 kg mass is located. The mass of the plate is represented by a 3 kg point mass at its centre.

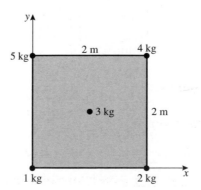

Figure 4.13

In this example the total mass M (in kilograms) is $1 + 2 + 4 + 5 + 3 = 15$.

The two formulae for $\bar{x}$ and $\bar{y}$ can be combined into one using column vector notation:

$$\begin{bmatrix} M\bar{x} \\ M\bar{y} \end{bmatrix} = \begin{bmatrix} \Sigma m_i\, x_i \\ \Sigma m_i\, y_i \end{bmatrix}$$

which is equivalent to $\quad M\begin{pmatrix} \bar{x} \\ \bar{y} \end{pmatrix} = \Sigma m_i \begin{pmatrix} x_i \\ y_i \end{pmatrix}$

Substituting our values for M and m_i and x_i and y_i:

$$15\begin{pmatrix} \bar{x} \\ \bar{y} \end{pmatrix} = 1\begin{pmatrix} 0 \\ 0 \end{pmatrix} + 2\begin{pmatrix} 2 \\ 0 \end{pmatrix} + 4\begin{pmatrix} 2 \\ 2 \end{pmatrix} + 5\begin{pmatrix} 0 \\ 2 \end{pmatrix} + 3\begin{pmatrix} 1 \\ 1 \end{pmatrix}$$

$$15\begin{pmatrix} \bar{x} \\ \bar{y} \end{pmatrix} = \begin{pmatrix} 15 \\ 21 \end{pmatrix}$$

$$\begin{pmatrix} \bar{x} \\ \bar{y} \end{pmatrix} = \begin{pmatrix} 1 \\ 1.4 \end{pmatrix}$$

The centre of mass is at the point $(1, 1.4)$.

EXAMPLE 4.7

Figure 4.14 shows a square table of side 2 m which is supported by four legs, each 1 m high, situated at the corners of a 1 m square. The mass of each leg is 1 kg and that of the table top 2 kg. The legs and the top are uniform. A small heavy object of mass 6 kg is placed on one corner of the table.

(i) Find the position of the centre of mass relative to the point O shown in the diagram using the axes indicated with unit length 1 m.

(ii) What is the significance of your result?

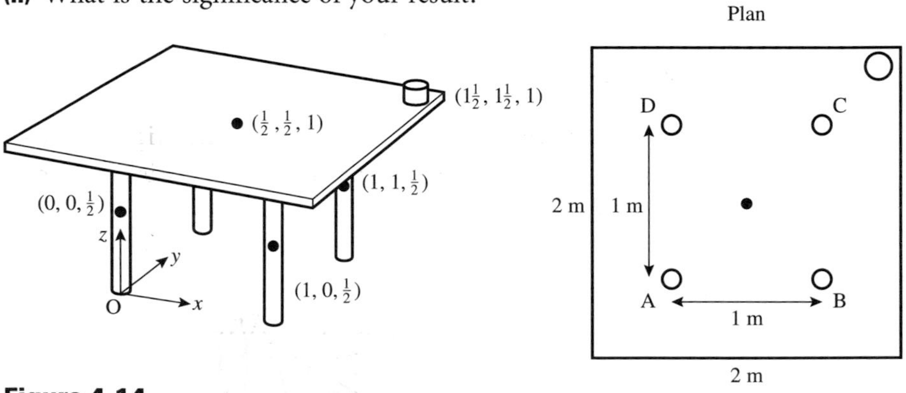

Figure 4.14

SOLUTION

(i) Let the co-ordinates of the centre of mass be $(\bar{x}, \bar{y}, \bar{z})$.

You can put the information in a table and then write the equations in vectors as below, or deal with each co-ordinate separately.

	leg A	leg B	leg C	leg D	table top	object	whole
mass	1	1	1	1	2	6	12
x	0	1	1	0	$\frac{1}{2}$	$1\frac{1}{2}$	$\bar{x}$
y	0	0	1	1	$\frac{1}{2}$	$1\frac{1}{2}$	$\bar{y}$
z	$\frac{1}{2}$	$\frac{1}{2}$	$\frac{1}{2}$	$\frac{1}{2}$	1	1	$\bar{z}$

Taking moments about O:

$$12 \times \begin{pmatrix} \bar{x} \\ \bar{y} \\ \bar{z} \end{pmatrix} = 1 \overset{A}{\begin{pmatrix} 0 \\ 0 \\ \frac{1}{2} \end{pmatrix}} + 1 \overset{B}{\begin{pmatrix} 1 \\ 0 \\ \frac{1}{2} \end{pmatrix}} + 1 \overset{C}{\begin{pmatrix} 1 \\ 1 \\ \frac{1}{2} \end{pmatrix}} + 1 \overset{D}{\begin{pmatrix} 0 \\ 1 \\ \frac{1}{2} \end{pmatrix}}$$

$$+ 2 \begin{pmatrix} \frac{1}{2} \\ \frac{1}{2} \\ 1 \end{pmatrix} + 6 \begin{pmatrix} 1\frac{1}{2} \\ 1\frac{1}{2} \\ 1 \end{pmatrix}$$

$$\Rightarrow 12 \begin{pmatrix} \bar{x} \\ \bar{y} \\ \bar{z} \end{pmatrix} = \begin{pmatrix} 12 \\ 12 \\ 10 \end{pmatrix}$$

$\Rightarrow$ The centre of mass is at $(1, 1, 0.83)$.

(ii) This means that the centre of mass is in the leg nearest the object and so the table is on the point of toppling over. All the weight is being taken by that one leg.

EXAMPLE 4.8

A metal disc of radius 15 cm has a hole of radius 5 cm cut in it as shown in figure 4.15. Find the centre of mass of the disc.

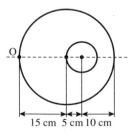

Figure 4.15

SOLUTION

Think of the original uncut disc as a composite body made up of the final body and a disc to fit into the hole. Since the material is uniform the mass of each part is proportional to its area.

The uncut disc = the final body + the cut out disc

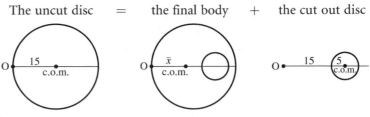

Figure 4.16

Area	$15^2\pi = 225\pi$	$15^2\pi - 5^2\pi = 200\pi$	$5^2\pi = 25\pi$
Distance from O to centre of mass	15 cm	$\bar{x}$ cm	20 cm

Taking moments about O

$$225\pi \times 15 = 200\pi \times \bar{x} + 25\pi \times 20$$

$$\Rightarrow \qquad \bar{x} = \frac{225 \times 15 - 25 \times 20}{200}$$

Divide by π

$$= 14.375$$

The centre of mass is 14.4 cm from O, that is 0.6 cm to the left of the centre of the disc.

1 Find the centre of mass of the following sets of point masses.

(i)   **(ii)**

(iii)   **(iv)**

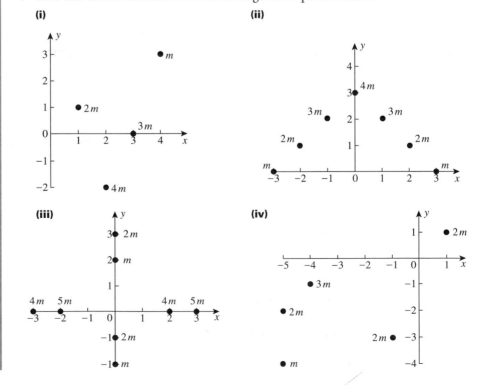

2 Masses of 1, 2, 3 and 4 grams are placed at the corners A, B, C and D of a square piece of uniform cardboard of side 10 cm and mass 5 g. Find the position of the centre of mass relative to axes through AB and AD.

3 As part of a Christmas lights display, letters are produced by mounting bulbs in holders 30 cm apart on light wire frames. The combined mass of a bulb and its holder is 200 g. Find the position of the centre of mass for each of the letters shown below, in terms of its horizontal and vertical displacement from the bottom left hand corner of the letter.

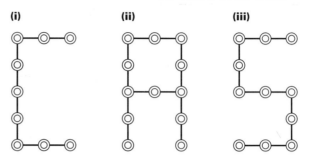

4 Four people of masses 60 kg, 65 kg, 62 kg and 75 kg sit on the four seats of the fairground ride shown below. The seats and the connecting arms are light. Find the radius of the circle described by the centre of mass when the ride rotates about O.

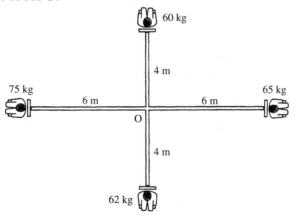

5 The following shapes are made out of uniform card.

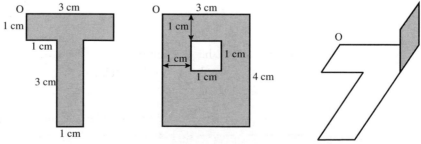

(i) For each shape find the co-ordinates of the centre of mass relative to O.

(ii) The right-hand square of the T shape is now bent up so that it is at right angles to the remainder. Where is the new centre of mass?

6 A filing cabinet has the dimensions shown in the diagram. The body of the cabinet has mass 20 kg and its construction is such that its centre of mass is at a height of 60 cm, and is 25 cm from the back of the cabinet. The mass of a drawer and its contents may be taken to be 10 kg and its centre of mass to be 10 cm above its base and 10 cm from its front face.

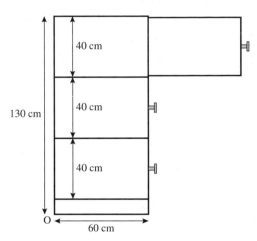

(i) Find the position of the centre of mass when all the drawers are closed.

(ii) Find the position of the centre of mass when the top two drawers are fully open.

(iii) Show that when all three drawers are fully opened the filing cabinet will tip over.

(iv) Two drawers are fully open. How far can the third one be opened without the cabinet tipping over?

7 A bird table is made from a uniform square base of side 0.3 m with mass 5 kg, a uniform square top of side 0.5 m and mass 2 kg, and a uniform thin rod of length 1.6 m and mass 1 kg connecting the centre of the top and base. The top and base have negligible thickness.

(i) Calculate the position of the centre of mass of the bird table.

(ii) At what angle can the bird table be turned about an edge of the base before it will topple?

It is decided to make the base heavier so that the bird table can be tipped at 40° to the horizontal before it topples. The base still has negligible thickness.

(iii) Show that the centre of mass must now be about 0.18 m above the base.

(iv) What is the new mass of the base?

[MEI]

8 Uniform wooden bricks have length 20 cm and height 5 cm. They are glued together as shown in the diagram with each brick 5 cm to the right of the one below it. The origin is taken to be at O.

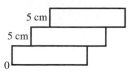

(i) Find the co-ordinates of the centre of mass for
     (a) 1 (b) 2 (c) 3 (d) 4 (e) 5 bricks.
(ii) How many bricks is it possible to assemble in this way without them tipping over?
(iii) If the displacement is changed from 5 cm to 2 cm find the co-ordinates of the centre of mass for n bricks. How many bricks can now be assembled?
(iv) If the displacement is $\frac{1}{2}$ cm, what is the maximum height possible for the centre of mass of such an assembly of bricks without them tipping over?

9 A pendant is made from a uniform circular disc of mass $4m$ and radius 2 cm with a decorative edging of mass m as shown. The centre of mass of the decoration is 1 cm below the centre, O, of the disc. The pendant is symmetrical about the diameter AB.

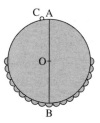

(i) Find the position of the centre of mass of the pendant.

The pendant should be hung from A but the light ring for hanging it is attached at C where angle AOC is 10°.
(ii) Find the angle between AB and the vertical when the pendant is hung from C.

10 A uniform rectangular lamina, ABCD, where AB is of length a and BC of length $2a$, has a mass $10m$. Further point masses m, $2m$, $3m$ and $4m$ are fixed to the points A, B, C and D, respectively.
(i) Find the centre of mass of the system relative to x and y axes along AB and AD respectively.
(ii) If the lamina is suspended from the point A find the angle that the diagonal AC makes with the vertical.
(iii) To what must the mass at point D be altered if this diagonal is to hang vertically?

[MEI]

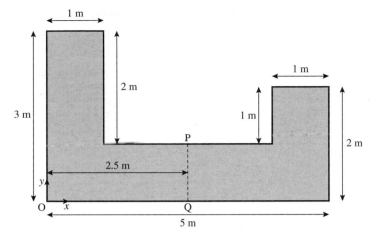

11

The diagram gives the dimensions of the design of a uniform metal plate. Using a co-ordinate system with O as origin, the x and y axes as shown and 1 metre as 1 unit,

(i) show that the centre of mass has y co-ordinate 1 and find its x co-ordinate.

The design requires the plate to have its centre of mass half-way across (i.e. on the line PQ in the diagram), and in order to achieve this a circular hole centred on $(\frac{1}{2}, \frac{1}{2})$ is considered.

(ii) Find the appropriate radius for such a hole and explain why this idea is not feasible.

It is then decided to cut two circular holes each of radius r, both centred on the line $x = \frac{1}{2}$. The first hole is centred at $(\frac{1}{2}, \frac{1}{2})$ and the centre of mass of the plate is to be at P.

(iii) Find the value of r and the co-ordinates of the centre of the second hole.

[MEI]

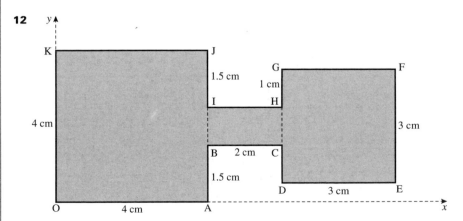

12

The diagram shows a lamina cut from a uniform sheet with dimensions as shown. OAJK, BCHI and DEFG are rectangular.

(i) Calculate the position of the centre of mass of the lamina referred to the axes shown in the diagram above. Give your answers correct to two decimal places.

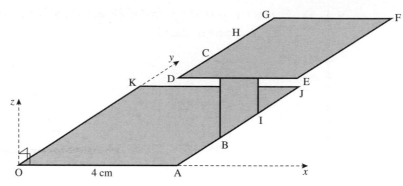

The lamina is folded along BI and CH to give the shape shown in the diagram above. BIHC is perpendicular to the plane OAJK and DEFG is parallel to the plane OAJK.

(ii) Calculate the position of the centre of mass of the folded lamina referred to the axes shown in the diagram above. Give your answers correct to two decimal places. The folded lamina is placed on a horizontal table with the edges ABIJ and EF in contact with the table. The diagram below shows this situation in elevation, looking in the y direction.

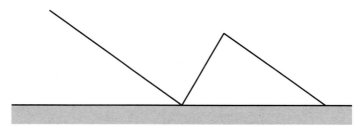

(iii) Is the folded lamina stable in this position? Your answer should be supported by appropriate calculations.

[**MEI**]

13

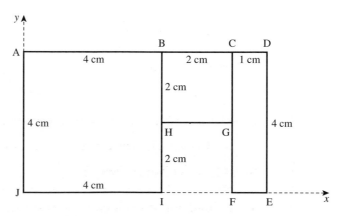

A uniform, thin, heavy plate is made up as shown in the diagram above from rectangular sections.

(i) Find the position of the centre of mass of the plate referred to the axes shown.

The rectangle CDEF is folded along CG so that it is perpendicular to the remaining part of the plate.

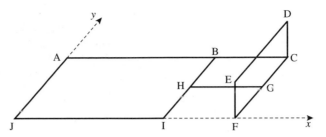

(ii) Find the x and y co-ordinates of the centre of mass of the whole plate bent in this way.

A further fold is made along BH so that BCGH is perpendicular to ABIJ (CDEF is now parallel to ABIJ).

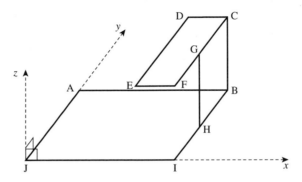

(iii) Find the x, y, and z co-ordinates of the centre of mass of the whole plate bent in this way.

[MEI]

14 (A)   **(B)**   **(C)**

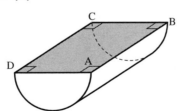

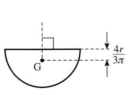

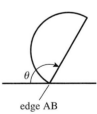

edge AB

A uniform solid with constant semi-circular cross-section of radius r is shown in figure (A). The centre of mass G of this solid is a distance $\dfrac{4r}{3\pi}$ from the rectangular face as shown in figure (B).

(i) The solid is placed on a rough horizontal table with the rectangular face inclined at θ to the horizontal, as shown in figure (C). When $\theta < 90°$ the curved surface is in contact with the table and when $\theta > 90°$ the edge AB rests on the table. Explain briefly why the solid rolls back for some values of θ, but for other values it tips over onto the rectangular face. Find the values of θ for which these cases occur.

(D)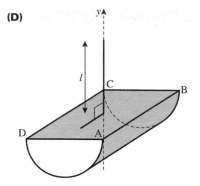

(E)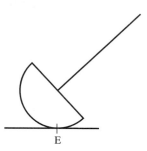

A cylindrical hole is drilled into the solid in the centre of the rectangular face and perpendicular to it. A cylindrical rod made of the same material as the solid and with the same radius as the hole completely fills the hole and has a further length l extending from the surface of the solid, as shown in figure (D). The mass of the solid is M and the mass per unit length of the rod is λ.

(ii) Show that the distance, $\bar{y}$, of the centre of mass of the composite body above the rectangular face ABCD is given by

$$\bar{y} = \frac{3\pi\lambda l^2 - 8rM}{6\pi(M + \lambda l)}$$

The composite body is placed on a rough table as shown in figure (E). Draw diagrams to show its position a few minutes later in the following cases. Give reasons for your answers.

(iii) $\bar{y} = 0$ **(iv)** $\bar{y} > 0$

[MEI]

15 A drink can is cylindrical, with height h cm, and when empty its mass is m g. The drink that fills it has mass M g and can be taken to fill the can completely.

(i) Find the height of the centre of mass when the can is standing on a level table and

    (a) is half full   **(b)** a proportion, α, of the drink remains.

When the can is full the centre of mass is clearly half-way up it, at height $\frac{1}{2}h$. The same is true when it is completely empty. In between these two extremes, the centre of mass is below the middle.

Show that when the centre of mass is at its minimum height

(i) $M\alpha^2 = m - 2\alpha m$

(ii) the centre of mass lies on the surface of the drink.
    [Hint: eliminate M.]

1 **Bridge**

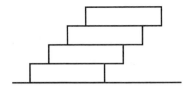

Figure 4.17

A bridge is made by placing identical bricks on top of each other as shown in the diagram. No glue or cement is used. How far can the bridge be extended without toppling over? You may use as many bricks as you like but only one is allowed at each level.

2 **Finding the centre of mass**

Collect a number of flat (but not necessarily uniform) objects, and investigate, for each of them, which is the most accurate method of determining its centre of mass.

(i) Calculation.

(ii) Balancing it on a pin.

(iii) Hanging it from two (or more) corners.

(iv) Balancing it on the edge of a table in a number of different orientations.

KEY POINTS

1 The centre of mass of a body has the property that:
the moment, about any point, of the whole mass of the body taken at the centre of mass is equal to the sum of the moments of the various particles comprising the body.

$$M\bar{\mathbf{r}} = \sum m_i \, \mathbf{r}_i \text{ where } M = \sum m_i$$

2 In one dimension

$$M\bar{x} = \sum m_i \, x_i$$

3 In two dimensions

$$M\begin{pmatrix} \bar{x} \\ \bar{y} \end{pmatrix} = \sum m_i \begin{pmatrix} x_i \\ y_i \end{pmatrix}$$

4 In three dimensions

$$M\begin{pmatrix} \bar{x} \\ \bar{y} \\ \bar{z} \end{pmatrix} = \sum m_i \begin{pmatrix} x_i \\ y_i \\ z_i \end{pmatrix}$$

5

Energy, work and power

I like work: it fascinates me. I can sit and look at it for hours.

Jerome K. Jerome

M C Escher's 'Waterfall'
© 2000 Cordon Art B.V. – Baarn –
Holland. All rights reserved.

This is a picture of a perpetual motion machine. What does this term mean and will this one work?

Energy and momentum

When describing the motion of objects in everyday language the words *energy* and *momentum* are often used quite loosely and sometimes no distinction is made between them. In mechanics they must be defined precisely.

For an object of mass *m* moving with velocity **v**:

- *Kinetic energy* $= \frac{1}{2}mv^2$ (this is the energy it has due to its motion)
- *Momentum* $= m\mathbf{v}$

Notice that kinetic energy is a scalar quantity with magnitude only, but momentum is a vector in the same direction as the velocity.

Both the kinetic energy and the momentum are liable to change when a force acts on a body and you will learn more about how the energy is changed in this chapter. You will meet momentum again in Chapter 6.

Work and energy

In everyday life you encounter many forms of energy such as heat, light, electricity and sound. You are familiar with the conversion of one form of energy to another: from chemical energy stored in wood to heat energy when you burn it; from electrical energy to the energy of a train's motion, and so on. The S.I. unit for energy is the joule, J.

Mechanical energy and work

In mechanics two forms of energy are particularly important.

Kinetic energy is the energy which a body possesses because of its motion.

- *The kinetic energy of a moving object* $= \frac{1}{2} \times mass \times (speed)^2$.

Potential energy is the energy which a body possesses because of its position. It may be thought of as stored energy which can be converted into kinetic or other forms of energy. You will meet this again on page 91.

The energy of an object is usually changed when it is acted on by a force. When a force is applied to an object which moves in the direction of its line of action, the force is said to do *work*. For a constant force this is defined as follows.

- *The work done by a constant force* = *force* × *distance moved in the direction of the force.*

The following examples illustrate how to use these ideas.

EXAMPLE 5.1

A brick, initially at rest, is raised by a force averaging 40 N to a height 5 m above the ground where it is left stationary. How much work is done by the force?

SOLUTION

The work done by the force raising the brick is

$$40 \times 5 = 200 \, \text{J}.$$

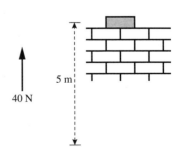

Figure 5.1

Examples 5.2 and 5.3 show how the work done by a force can be related to the change in kinetic energy of an object.

A train travelling on level ground is subject to a resisting force (from the brakes and air resistance) of 250 kN for a distance of 5 km. How much kinetic energy does the train lose?

SOLUTION

The forward force is –250 000 N.

> Work and energy have the same units

The work done by it is $-250\,000 \times 5000 = -1\,250\,000\,000$ J.

Hence $-1\,250\,000\,000$ J of kinetic energy are gained by the train, in other words $+1\,250\,000\,000$ J of kinetic energy are lost and the train slows down. This energy is converted to other forms such as heat and perhaps a little sound.

A car of mass m kg is travelling at u ms^{-1} when the driver applies a constant driving force of F N. The ground is level and the road is straight and air resistance can be ignored. The driving force will have an effect on the speed of the car. Suppose it increases to v ms^{-1} in a period of t s over a distance of s m.

Treating the car as a particle and applying Newton's second law:

$$F = ma$$

$$a = \frac{F}{m}$$

Since F is assumed constant, the acceleration is constant also so using $v^2 = u^2 + 2as$

$$v^2 = u^2 + \frac{2Fs}{m}$$

$$\Rightarrow \quad \tfrac{1}{2}mv^2 = \tfrac{1}{2}mu^2 + Fs$$

$$Fs = \tfrac{1}{2}mv^2 - \tfrac{1}{2}mu^2$$

Thus

- *work done by force = final kinetic energy – initial kinetic energy* of car.

The work–energy principle

Examples 5.4 and 5.5 illustrate the *work–energy principle* which states that:

- *The total work done by the forces acting on a body is equal to the increase in the kinetic energy of the body.*

EXAMPLE 5.4

A sledge of total mass 30 kg, initially moving at $2\,\text{ms}^{-1}$, is pulled 14 m across smooth horizontal ice by a horizontal rope in which there is a constant tension of 45 N. Find its final velocity.

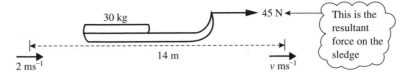

This is the resultant force on the sledge

Figure 5.2

SOLUTION

Since the ice is smooth, the work done by the force is all converted into kinetic energy and the final velocity can be found using

work done by the force = final kinetic energy − initial kinetic energy
$$45 \times 14 = \tfrac{1}{2} \times 30 \times v^2 - \tfrac{1}{2} \times 30 \times 2^2$$

Giving $v^2 = 46$ and the final velocity of the sledge as $6.8\,\text{ms}^{-1}$.

EXAMPLE 5.5

The combined mass of a cyclist and her bicycle is 65 kg. She accelerated from rest to $8\,\text{ms}^{-1}$ in 80 m along a horizontal road.

(i) Calculate the work done by the net force in accelerating the cyclist and her bicycle.

(ii) Hence calculate the net forward force (assuming the force to be constant).

SOLUTION

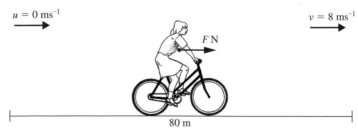

Figure 5.3

(i) The work done by the net force F is given by

$$\text{work} = \text{final K.E.} - \text{initial K.E.}$$
$$= \tfrac{1}{2}mv^2 - \tfrac{1}{2}mu^2$$
$$= \tfrac{1}{2} \times 65 \times 8^2 - 0$$
$$= 2080\,\text{J}$$

The work done is 2080 J.

(ii)   Work done $= Fs$
$$= F \times 80$$
So $80F = 2080$
$$F = 26$$

The net forward force is 26 N.

Work

It is important to realise that:

- work is done by a force
- work is only done when there is movement
- a force only does work on an object when it has a component in the direction of motion of the object.

It is quite common to speak of the work done by a person, say in pushing a lawn mower. In fact this is the work done by the force of the person on the lawn mower.

Notice that if you stand holding a brick stationary above your head, painful though it may be, the force you are exerting on it is doing no work. Nor is this vertical force doing any work if you walk round the room keeping the brick at the same height. However, once you start climbing the stairs, a component of the brick's movement is in the direction of the upward force that you are exerting on it, so the force is now doing some work.

When applying the work–energy principle, you have to be careful to include *all* the forces acting on the body. In the example of a brick of weight 40 N being raised 5 m vertically, starting and ending at rest, the change in kinetic energy is clearly 0.

This seems paradoxical when it is clear that the force which raised the brick has done $40 \times 5 = 200$ J of work. However, the brick was subject to another force, namely its weight, which did $-40 \times 5 = -200$ J of work on it, giving a total of $200 + (-200) = 0$ J.

Conservation of mechanical energy

The net forward force on the cyclist in Example 5.5 is the girl's driving force minus resistive forces such as air resistance and friction in the bearings. In the absence of such resistive forces, she would gain more kinetic energy; also the work she does against them is lost, it is dissipated as heat and sound. Contrast this with the work a cyclist does against gravity when going uphill. This work can be recovered as kinetic energy on a downhill run. The work done against the force of gravity is conserved and gives the cyclist potential energy (see page 91).

Forces such as friction which result in the dissipation of mechanical energy are called *dissipative forces*. Forces which conserve mechanical energy are called *conservative forces*. The force of gravity is a conservative force and so is the tension in an elastic string; you can test this using an elastic band.

$$\text{Work done by resistance force} + 12\,000 \times 10^6 = 855 \times 10^6$$
$$\text{Work done by resistance force} = -11\,145 \times 10^6 \, \text{J}$$
$$\text{Average force} \times \text{distance} = \text{work done by force}$$
$$\text{Average force} \times 30\,000 = -11\,145 \times 10^6$$

$\Rightarrow$ The average resistance force is 371 500 N (in the negative direction).

Note

When an aircraft is in flight, most of the work done by the resistance force results in air currents and the generation of heat. A typical large jet cruising at 35 000 feet has a body temperature about 30°C above the surrounding air temperature. For supersonic flight the temperature difference is much greater. Concorde flies with a skin temperature more than 200°C above that of the surrounding air.

EXERCISE 5A

1 Find the kinetic energy of the following objects.
   (i)   An ice skater of mass 50 kg travelling with speed $10 \, \text{ms}^{-1}$.
   (ii) An elephant of mass 5 tonnes moving at $4 \, \text{ms}^{-1}$.
   (iii) A train of mass 7000 tonnes travelling at $40 \, \text{ms}^{-1}$.
   (iv) The moon, mass 7.4×10^{22} kg, travelling at $1000 \, \text{ms}^{-1}$ in its orbit round the earth.
   (v)   A bacterium of mass 2×10^{-16} g which has speed $1 \, \text{mm s}^{-1}$.

2 Find the work done by a man in the following situations.
   (i)   He pushes a packing case of mass 35 kg a distance of 5 m across a rough floor against a resistance of 200 N. The case starts and finishes at rest.
   (ii) He pushes a packing case of mass 35 kg a distance of 5 m across a rough floor against a resistance force of 200 N. The case starts at rest and finishes with a speed of $2 \, \text{ms}^{-1}$.
   (iii) He pushes a packing case of mass 35 kg a distance of 5 m across a rough floor against a resistance force of 200 N. Initially the case has speed $2 \, \text{ms}^{-1}$ but it ends at rest.
   (iv) He is handed a packing case of mass 35 kg. He holds it stationary, at the same height, for 20 s and then someone else takes it from him.

3 A sprinter of mass 60 kg is at rest at the beginning of a race and accelerates to $12 \, \text{ms}^{-1}$ in a distance of 30 m. Assume air resistance to be negligible.
   (i)   Calculate the kinetic energy of the sprinter at the end of the 30 m.
   (ii) Write down the work done by the sprinter over this distance.
   (iii) Calculate the forward force exerted by the sprinter, assuming it to be constant, using work = force × distance.
   (iv) Using force = mass × acceleration and the constant acceleration formulae, show that this force is consistent with the sprinter having speed $12 \, \text{ms}^{-1}$ after 30 m.

4 A sports car of mass 1.2 tonnes accelerates from rest to $30 \, \text{ms}^{-1}$ in a distance of 150 m. Assume air resistance to be negligible.

(i) Calculate the work done in accelerating the car. Does your answer depend on an assumption that the driving force is constant?

(ii) If the driving force is in fact constant, what is its magnitude?

5 A car of mass 1600 kg is travelling at speed $25 \, \text{ms}^{-1}$ when the brakes are applied so that it stops after moving a further 75 m.

(i) Find the work done by the brakes.

(ii) Find the retarding force from the brakes, assuming that it is constant and that other resistive forces may be neglected.

6 The forces acting on a hot air balloon of mass 500 kg are its weight and the total uplift force.

(i) Find the total work done when the speed of the balloon changes from

 (a) $2 \, \text{ms}^{-1}$ to $5 \, \text{ms}^{-1}$ (b) $8 \, \text{ms}^{-1}$ to $3 \, \text{ms}^{-1}$

(ii) If the balloon rises 100 m vertically while its speed changes calculate in each case the work done by the uplift force.

7 A bullet of mass 20 g, found at the scene of a police investigation, had penetrated 16 cm into a wooden post. The speed for that type of bullet is known to be $80 \, \text{ms}^{-1}$.

(i) Find the kinetic energy of the bullet before it entered the post.

(ii) What happened to this energy when the bullet entered the wooden post?

(iii) Write down the work done in stopping the bullet.

(iv) Calculate the resistive force on the bullet, assuming it to be constant.

Another bullet of the same mass and shape had clearly been fired from a different and unknown type of gun. This bullet had penetrated 20 cm into the post.

(v) Estimate the speed of this bullet before it hit the post.

8 The Highway Code gives the braking distance for a car travelling at $22 \, \text{ms}^{-1}$ (50 mph) to be 38 m (125 ft). A car of mass 1300 kg is brought to rest in just this distance. It may be assumed that the only resistance forces come from the car's brakes.

(i) Find the work done by the brakes.

(ii) Find the average force exerted by the brakes.

(iii) What happened to the kinetic energy of the car?

(iv) What happens when you drive a car with the handbrake on?

9 A car of mass 1200 kg experiences a constant resistance force of 600 N. The driving force from the engine depends upon the gear, as shown in the table.

Gear	1	2	3	4
Force (N)	2800	2100	1400	1000

Starting from rest, the car is driven 20 m in first gear, 40 m in second, 80 m in third and 100 m in fourth. How fast is the car travelling at the end?

10 In this question take g to be $10\,\text{ms}^{-2}$. A chest of mass $60\,\text{kg}$ is resting on a rough horizontal floor. The coefficient of friction between the floor and the chest is 0.4. A woman pushes the chest in such a way that its speed–time graph is as shown below.

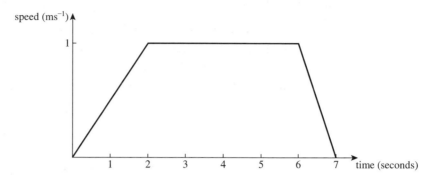

(i) Find the force of frictional resistance acting on the chest when it moves.

(ii) Use the speed–time graph to find the total distance travelled by the chest.

(iii) Find the total work done by the woman.

(iv) Find the acceleration of the chest in the first 2 s of its motion and hence the force exerted by the woman during this time, and the work done.

(v) In the same way find the work done by the woman during the time intervals 2 to 6 s, and 6 to 7 s.

(vi) Show that your answers to parts (iv) and (v) are consistent with your answer to part (iii).

Gravitational potential energy

As you have seen, kinetic energy (K.E.) is the energy that an object has because of its motion. Potential energy (P.E.) is the energy an object has because of its position. The units of potential energy are the same as those of kinetic energy or any other form of energy, namely joules.

One form of potential energy is *gravitational potential energy*. The gravitational potential energy of the object in figure 5.6 of mass m kg at height h m above a fixed reference level, O, is mgh J. If it falls to the reference level, the force of gravity does mgh J of work and the body loses mgh J of potential energy.

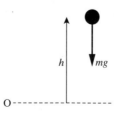

Figure 5.6

A loss in gravitational potential energy is an alternative way of accounting for the work done by the force of gravity.

If a mass m kg is *raised* through a distance h m, the gravitational potential energy *increases* by mgh J. If a mass m kg is lowered through a distance h m the gravitational potential energy *decreases* by mgh J.

EXAMPLE 5.8

Calculate the gravitational potential energy, relative to the ground, of a ball of mass 0.15 kg at a height of 2 m above the ground.

SOLUTION

Mass $m = 0.15$, height $h = 2$.

$$\text{Gravitational potential energy} = mgh$$
$$= 0.15 \times 9.8 \times 2$$
$$= 2.94 \text{ J.}$$

Note

If the ball falls:

$$\text{loss in P.E.} = \text{work done by gravity}$$
$$= \text{gain in K.E.}$$

There is no change in the total energy (P.E. + K.E.) of the ball.

Using conservation of mechanical energy

When gravity is the only force which does work on a body, mechanical energy is conserved. When this is the case, many problems are easily solved using energy. This is possible even when the acceleration is not constant.

EXAMPLE 5.9

A skier slides down a smooth ski slope 400 m long which is at an angle of 30° to the horizontal. Find the speed of the skier when he reaches the bottom of the slope.

At the foot of the slope the ground becomes horizontal and is made rough in order to help him to stop. The coefficient of friction between his skis and the ground is $\frac{1}{4}$.

(i) Find how far the skier travels before coming to rest.
(ii) In what way is your model unrealistic?

SOLUTION

The skier is modelled as a particle.

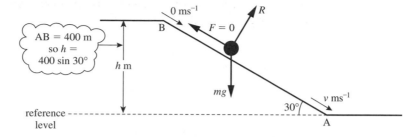

Figure 5.7

(i) Since in this case the slope is smooth, the frictional force is zero. The skier is subject to two external forces, his weight mg and the normal reaction from the slope.

The normal reaction between the skier and the slope does no work because the skier does not move in the direction of this force. The only force which does work is gravity, so mechanical energy is conserved.

$$\text{Total mechanical energy at B} = mgh + \tfrac{1}{2}mu^2$$
$$= m \times 9.8 \times 400 \sin 30° + 0$$
$$= 1960m \, \text{J}$$
$$\text{Total mechanical energy at A} = (0 + \tfrac{1}{2}mv^2) \, \text{J}$$

Since mechanical energy is conserved,

$$\tfrac{1}{2}mv^2 = 1960m \qquad\qquad ①$$
$$v^2 = 3920$$
$$v = 62.6$$

The skier's speed at the bottom of the slope is $62.6 \, \text{ms}^{-1}$.

Notice that the mass of the skier cancels out. Using this model, all skiers should arrive at the bottom of the slope with the same speed. Also the slope could be curved so long as the total height lost is the same.

For the horizontal part there is some friction. Suppose that the skier travels a further distance s m before stopping.

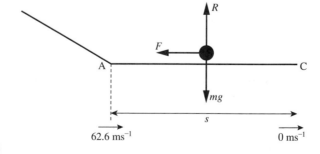

Figure 5.8

Coulomb's law of friction gives $\qquad F = \mu R = \tfrac{1}{4}R.$

Since there is no vertical acceleration we can also say $R = mg$

So $\qquad\qquad\qquad\qquad\qquad\qquad F = \tfrac{1}{4}mg.$

Work done by the friction force $F \times (-s) = -\frac{1}{4} mgs$.

> Negative because the motion is in the opposite direction to the force

The increase in kinetic energy between A and C $= (0 - \frac{1}{2} mv^2)$ J.

Using the work–energy principle

$$-\frac{1}{4} mgs = -\frac{1}{2} mv^2 = -1960m \text{ from } ①$$

Solving for s gives $s = 800$.

So the distance the skier travels before stopping is 800 m.

(ii) The assumptions made in solving this problem are that friction on the slope and air resistance are negligible, and that the slope ends in a smooth curve at A. Clearly the speed of 62.6 ms^{-1} is very high, so the assumption that friction and air resistance are negligible must be suspect.

EXAMPLE 5.10

Ama, whose mass is 40 kg, is taking part in an assault course. The obstacle shown in figure 5.9 is a river at the bottom of a ravine 8 m wide which she has to cross by swinging on a rope 5 m long secured to a point on the branch of a tree, immediately above the centre of the ravine.

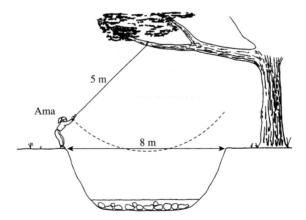

Figure 5.9

Find how fast Ama is travelling at the lowest point of her crossing:

(i) if she starts from rest

(ii) if she launches herself off at a speed of 1 ms^{-1}.

Will her speed be 1 ms^{-1} faster throughout her crossing?

SOLUTION

(i) The vertical height Ama loses is HB in the diagram.

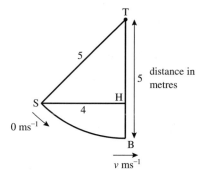

Figure 5.10

Using Pythagoras

$$TH = \sqrt{5^2 - 4^2} = 3$$
$$HB = 5 - 3 = 2$$
$$\text{P.E. lost} = mgh$$
$$= 40g \times 2$$
$$\text{K.E. gained} = \tfrac{1}{2}mv^2 - 0$$
$$= \tfrac{1}{2} \times 40 \times v^2$$

By conservation of energy, K.E. gained = P.E. lost

$$\tfrac{1}{2} \times 40 \times v^2 = 40 \times 9.8 \times 2$$
$$v = 6.26$$

Ama is travelling at $6.26\,\text{ms}^{-1}$.

(ii) If she has initial speed $1\,\text{ms}^{-1}$ at S and speed $v\,\text{ms}^{-1}$ at B, her initial K.E. is $\tfrac{1}{2} \times 40 \times 1^2$ J and her K.E. at B is $\tfrac{1}{2} \times 40 \times v^2$.

Using conservation of energy,

$$\tfrac{1}{2} \times 40 \times v^2 - \tfrac{1}{2} \times 40 \times 1^2 = 40 \times 9.8 \times 2$$

This gives $v = 6.34$, so Ama's speed at the lowest point is now $6.34\,\text{ms}^{-1}$, only $0.08\,\text{ms}^{-1}$ faster than in part (i), so she clearly will not travel $1\,\text{ms}^{-1}$ faster throughout.

Historical note

James Joule was born in Salford in Lancashire on Christmas Eve 1818. He studied at Manchester University at the same time as the famous chemist, Dalton.

Joule spent much of his life conducting experiments to measure the equivalence of heat and mechanical forms of energy to ever increasing degrees of accuracy. Working with Thompson, he also discovered that a gas cools when it expands without doing work against external forces. It was this discovery that paved the way for the development of refrigerators.

Joule died in 1889 but his contribution to science is remembered with the S.I. Unit for energy named after him.

Work and kinetic energy for two-dimensional motion

 Imagine that you are cycling along a level winding road in a strong wind. Suppose that the strength and direction of the wind are constant, but because the road is winding sometimes the wind is directly against you but at other times it is from your side.

How does the work you do in travelling a certain distance – say 1 m – change with your direction?

Work done by a force at an angle to the direction of motion

You have probably deduced that as a cyclist you would do work against the component of the wind force that is directly against you. The sideways component does not resist your forward progress.

Suppose that you are sailing and the angle between the force, F, of the wind on your sail and the direction of your motion is θ. In a certain time you travel a distance d in the direction of F, see figure 5.11, but during that time you actually travel a distance s along the line OP.

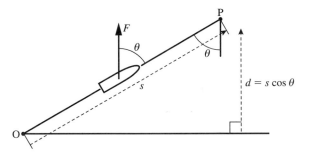

Figure 5.11

Work done by $F = Fd$

Since $d = s\cos\theta$, the work done by the force F is $Fs\cos\theta$. This can also be written as the product of the component of F along OP, $F\cos\theta$, and the distance moved along OP, s.

$$F \times s\cos\theta = F\cos\theta \times s$$

[Notice that the direction of F is not necessarily the same as the direction of the wind, it depends on how you have set your sails.]

EXAMPLE 5.11

5

Work and kinetic energy for two-dimensional motion

As a car of mass m kg drives up a slope at an angle α to the horizontal it experiences a constant resistive force F N and a driving force D N. What can be deduced about the work done by D as the car moves a distance d m uphill if:

(i) the car moves at constant speed?

(ii) the car slows down?

(iii) the car gains speed?

The initial and final speeds of the car are denoted by u ms^{-1} and v ms^{-1} respectively.

(iv) Write v^2 in terms of the other variables.

SOLUTION

The diagram shows the forces acting on the car. The table shows the work done by each force. The normal reaction, R, does no work as the car moves no distance in the direction of R.

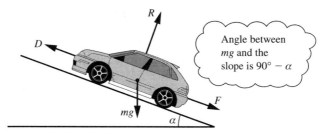

Angle between mg and the slope is $90° - \alpha$

Figure 5.12

Force	Work done
Resistance F	$-Fd$
Normal reaction R	0
Force of gravity mg	$-mgd \cos(90° - \alpha) = -mgd \sin \alpha$
Driving force D	Dd
Total work done	$Dd - Fd - mgd \sin \alpha$

(i) If the car moves at a constant speed there is no change in kinetic energy so the total work done is zero, giving

Work done by D is

$$Dd = Fd + mgd \sin \alpha.$$

(ii) If the car slows down the total work done by the forces is negative, hence

Work done by D is

$$Dd < Fd + mgd \sin \alpha.$$

(iii) If the car gains speed the total work done by the forces is positive

Work done by D is

$$Dd > Fd + mgd \sin \alpha.$$

(iv)   Total work done = final K.E. − initial K.E.

$$\Rightarrow \quad Dd - Fd - mgd \sin \alpha = \tfrac{1}{2} mv^2 - \tfrac{1}{2} mu^2$$

Multiplying by $\dfrac{2}{m}$

$$\Rightarrow \quad v^2 = u^2 + \frac{2d}{m}(D - F) - 2gd \sin \alpha$$

1 Calculate the gravitational potential energy, relative to the reference level OA, for each of the objects shown.

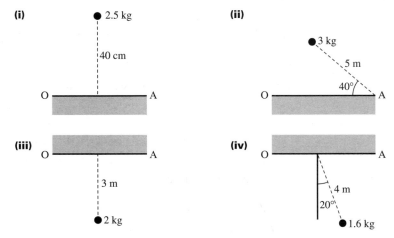

2 Calculate the change in gravitational potential energy when each object moves from A to B in the situations shown below. State whether the change is an increase or a decrease.

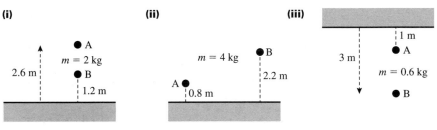

3 A vase of mass 1.2 kg is lifted from ground level and placed on a shelf at a height of 1.5 m. Find the work done against the force of gravity.

4 Find the increase in gravitational potential energy of a woman of mass 60 kg who climbs to the twelfth floor of a block of flats. The distance between floors is 3.3 m.

5 A car of mass 0.9 tonnes is driven 200 m up a slope inclined at 5° to the horizontal. There is a resistance force of 100 N.

  (i) Find the work done by the car against gravity.

  (ii) Find the work done against the resistance force.

  (iii) When asked to work out the total work done by the car, a student replied '$(900g + 100) \times 200$ J'. Explain the error in this answer.

  (iv) If the car slows down from $12\,\mathrm{ms}^{-1}$ to $8\,\mathrm{ms}^{-1}$, what is the total work done by the engine?

6 A sledge of mass 10 kg is being pulled across level ground by a rope which makes an angle of 20° with the horizontal. The tension in the rope is 80 N and there is a resistance force of 14 N.

  (i) Find the work done by

    (a) the tension in the rope

    (b) the resistance force while the sledge moves a distance of 20 m.

  (ii) Find the speed of the sledge after it has moved 20 m.

    (a) if it starts at rest   **(b)** if it starts at $4\,\mathrm{ms}^{-1}$.

7 A bricklayer carries a hod of bricks of mass 25 kg up a ladder of length 10 m inclined at an angle of 60° to the horizontal.

  (i) Calculate the increase in the gravitational potential energy of the bricks.

  (ii) If instead he had raised the bricks vertically to the same height, using a rope and pulleys, would the increase in potential energy be (a) less, (b) the same, or (c) more than in part (i)?

8 A girl of mass 45 kg slides down a smooth water chute of length 6 m inclined at an angle of 40° to the horizontal.

  (i) Find

    (a) the decrease in her potential energy

    (b) her speed at the bottom.

  (ii) How are answers to part (i) affected if the slide is not smooth?

9 A gymnast of mass 50 kg swings on a rope of length 10 m. Initially the rope makes an angle of 50° with the vertical.

  (i) Find the decrease in her potential energy when the rope has reached the vertical.

  (ii) Find her kinetic energy and hence her speed when the rope is vertical, assuming that air resistance may be neglected.

  (iii) The gymnast continues to swing. What angle will the rope make with the vertical when she is next temporarily at rest?

  (iv) Explain why the tension in the rope does no work.

10 A stone of mass 0.2 kg is dropped from the top of a building 78.4 m high. After t s it has fallen a distance x m and has speed v ms^{-1}.

  (i) What is the gravitational potential energy of the stone relative to ground level when it is at the top of the building?

  (ii) What is the potential energy of the stone t s later?

  (iii) Show that, for certain values of t, $v^2 = 19.6x$ and state the range of values of t for which it is true.

  (iv) Find the speed of the stone when it is half-way to the ground.

  (v) At what height will the stone have half its final speed?

11 Wesley, whose mass is 70 kg, inadvertently steps off a bridge 50 m above water. When he hits the water, Wesley is travelling at 25 ms^{-1}.

  (i) Calculate the potential energy Wesley has lost and the kinetic energy he has gained.

  (ii) Find the size of the resistance force acting on Wesley while he is in the air, assuming it to be constant.

Wesley descends to a depth of 5 m below the water surface, then returns to the surface.

  (iii) Find the total upthrust (assumed constant) acting on him while he is moving downwards in the water.

12 A hockey ball of mass 0.15 kg is hit from the centre of a pitch. Its position vector (in m), t s later is modelled by

$$\mathbf{r} = 10t\,\mathbf{i} + (10t - 4.9t^2)\,\mathbf{j}$$

where the unit vectors $\mathbf{i}$ and $\mathbf{j}$ are in directions along the line of the pitch and vertically upwards.

  (i) What value of g is used in this model?

  (ii) Find an expression for the gravitational potential energy of the ball at time t. For what values of t is your answer valid?

  (iii) What is the maximum height of the ball? What is its velocity at that instant?

  (iv) Find the initial velocity, speed and kinetic energy of the ball.

  (v) Show that according to this model mechanical energy is conserved and state what modelling assumption is implied by this. Is it reasonable in this context?

13 A ski-run starts at altitude 2471 m and ends at 1863 m.

  (i) If all resistance forces could be ignored, what would the speed of the skier be at the end of the run?

A particular skier of mass 70 kg actually attains a speed of 42 ms^{-1}. The length of the run is 3.1 km.

  (ii) Find the average force of resistance acting on a skier.

Two skiers are equally skilful.

  (iii) Which would you expect to be travelling faster by the end of the run, the heavier or the lighter?

14 A tennis ball of mass 0.06 kg is hit vertically upwards with speed 20 ms^{-1} from a point 1.1 m above the ground. It reaches a height of 16 m.

  (i) Find the initial kinetic energy of the ball, and its gain in potential energy when it is at its highest point

  (ii) Calculate the loss of mechanical energy due to air resistance.

  (iii) Find the magnitude of the air resistance force on the ball, assuming it to be constant while the ball is moving.

  (iv) With what speed does the ball land?

15

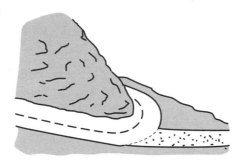

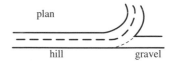

In this question take $g = 10$ ms^{-2}

Steep hills often have escape roads on sharp corners. These can be made of gravel which stops any vehicles out of control. Consider a model of such a situation where a vehicle starting from rest has free-wheeled down a hill which drops a vertical distance 20 m with no resistances to motion and, travelling horizontally, runs into the gravel, which is also horizontal.

Suppose the vehicle is a car of mass 800 kg.

  (i) What is the speed of the car when it reaches the gravel?

  (ii) Given that the car is brought to rest by the gravel in 10 m by a constant retarding force, show that the magnitude of this force is 16 kN.

Suppose the vehicle is a lorry of mass M tonnes that has gone out of control in the same way as the car so that it reaches the gravel at the same speed.

  (iii) If $M = 20$ and the lorry is subjected to the same constant retarding force as the car, find how far the lorry would go in the gravel before being brought to rest.

In fact, heavier vehicles sink further into the gravel, thereby increasing the retarding force. Given that the retarding force is directly proportional to the weight of the vehicle, and using the information that a vehicle of mass 800 kg is brought to rest in 10 m,

  (iv) find an expression for the retarding force for a vehicle of mass M tonnes

  (v) show that the distance required to bring a vehicle to rest is 10 m for any M.

[MEI]

16 Akosua draws water from a well 12 m below the ground. Her bucket holds 5 kg of water and by the time she has pulled it to the top of the well it is travelling at $1.2\,\mathrm{ms}^{-1}$.

(i) How much work does Akosua do in drawing the bucket of water?

On an average day 150 people in the village each draw six such buckets of water. One day a new electric pump is installed that takes water from the well and fills an overhead tank 5 m above ground level every morning. The flow rate through the pump is such that the water has speed $2\,\mathrm{ms}^{-1}$ on arriving in the tank.

(ii) Assuming that the villagers' demand for water remains unaltered, how much work does the pump do in one day?

It takes the pump one hour to fill the tank each morning.

(iii) At what rate does the pump do work, in joules per second (watts)?

17

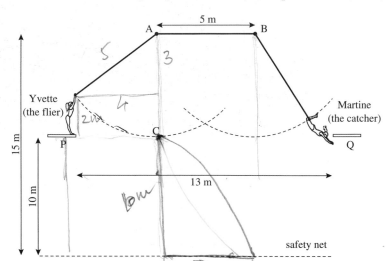

Yvette and Martine are trapeze artists in a circus. Their equipment is shown in the diagram. The trapezes are suspended from points A and B, 5 m apart but at the same height, 15 m above the safety net. The two platforms P and Q are at the same height, 10 m above the safety net, 13 m apart and placed symmetrically with respect to points A and B. C is level with P and Q.

Yvette, who is the 'flier', holds her trapeze while standing on the edge of platform P, with her arms straight above her. In this position her hands are 2 m above the platform.

(i) How long is the rope of Yvette's trapeze?

(ii) How fast is Yvette travelling when she passes the lowest point (C) of her trapeze's arc? (Assume she does not push herself off.)

As part of their act they frighten the audience. Yvette lets go of her trapeze at point C and Martine pretends to forget to catch her. Yvette falls into the safety net.

(iii) How far will Yvette move horizontally before her feet land in the net?

(iv) Describe, and comment on, the assumptions you have made in modelling this situation.

Power

It is claimed that a motorcycle engine can develop a maximum *power* of 26.5 kW at a top *speed* of 103 mph. This suggests that power is related to speed and this is indeed the case.

Power is the rate at which work is being done. A powerful car does work at a greater rate than a less powerful one.

You might find it helpful to think in terms of a force, F, acting for a very short time t over a small distance s. Assume F to be constant over this short time. Power is the rate of working so

$$\text{power} = \frac{\text{work}}{\text{time}}$$
$$= \frac{Fs}{t}$$
$$= Fv$$

> This gives you the power at an *instant* of time. The result is true whether or not F is constant

The power of a vehicle moving at speed v under a driving force F is given by Fv.

For a motor vehicle the power is produced by the engine, whereas for a bicycle it is produced by the cyclist. They both make the wheels turn, and the friction between the rotating wheels and the ground produces a forward force on the machine.

The unit of power is the watt (W), named after James Watt. The power produced by a force of 1 N acting on an object that is moving at $1\,\text{ms}^{-1}$ is 1 W. Because the watt is such a small unit you will probably use kilowatts more often ($1\,\text{kW} = 1000\,\text{W}$).

EXAMPLE 5.12

A car of mass 1000 kg can produce a maximum power of 45 kW. Its driver wishes to overtake another vehicle. Ignoring air resistance, find the maximum acceleration of the car when it is travelling at

(i) $12\,\text{ms}^{-1}$ **(ii)** $28\,\text{ms}^{-1}$ (these are about 27 mph and 63 mph).

SOLUTION

(i) Power = force × velocity
The driving force at $12\,\text{ms}^{-1}$ is F_1 N where

$$45\,000 = F_1 \times 12$$
$$\Rightarrow \qquad F_1 = 3750.$$

By Newton's second law $F = ma$

$$\Rightarrow \qquad \text{acceleration} = \frac{3750}{1000} = 3.75\,\text{ms}^{-2}.$$

(ii) Now the driving force F_2 is given by

$$45\,000 = F_2 \times 28$$
$$\Rightarrow \qquad F_2 = 1607$$
$$\Rightarrow \qquad \text{acceleration} = \frac{1607}{1000} = 1.61\,\text{ms}^{-2}.$$

This example shows why it is easier to overtake a slow moving vehicle.

EXAMPLE 5.13

A car of mass 900 kg produces power 45 kW when moving at a constant speed. It experiences a resistance of 1700 N.

(i) What is its speed?
(ii) The car comes to a downhill stretch inclined at $2°$ to the horizontal. What is its maximum speed downhill if the power and resistance remain unchanged?

SOLUTION

(i) As the car is travelling at a constant speed, there is no resultant force on the car. In this case the forward force of the engine must have the same magnitude as the resistance forces, i.e. 1700 N.

Denoting the speed of the car by $v\,\mathrm{ms}^{-1}$, $P = Fv$ gives

$$v = \frac{P}{F}$$
$$= \frac{45\,000}{1700}$$
$$= 26.5.$$

The speed of the car is $26.5\,\mathrm{ms}^{-1}$ (approximately 60 mph).

(ii) The diagram shows the forces acting.

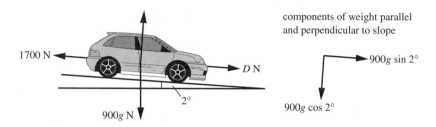

Figure 5.13

At maximum speed there is no acceleration so the resultant force down the slope is zero.

When the driving force is $D\,\mathrm{N}$

$$D + 900g \sin 2° - 1700 = 0$$
$$\Rightarrow \qquad\qquad\qquad\qquad D = 1392$$

But power is Dv so $\qquad 45\,000 = 1392v$

$$\Rightarrow \quad v = \frac{45\,000}{1392}$$

The maximum speed is $32.3\,\mathrm{ms}^{-1}$ (about 73 mph).

Historical note

James Watt was born in 1736 in Greenock in Scotland, the son of a house- and ship-builder. As a boy James was frail and he was taught by his mother rather than going to school. This allowed him to spend time in his father's workshop where he developed practical and inventive skills.

As a young man he manufactured mathematical instruments: quadrants, scales, compasses and so on. One day he was repairing a model steam engine for a friend and noticed that its design was very wasteful of steam. He proposed an alternative arrangement, which was to become standard on later steam engines. This was the first of many engineering inventions which made possible the subsequent industrial revolution. James Watt died in 1819, a well known and highly respected man. His name lives on as the S.I. unit for power.

1 A builder hoists bricks up to the top of the house he is building. Each brick weighs 3.5 kg and the house is 9 m high. In the course of one hour the builder raises 120 bricks from ground level to the top of the house, where they are unloaded by his mate.

   (i) Find the increase in gravitational potential energy of one brick when it is raised in this way.

   (ii) Find the total work done by the builder in one hour of raising bricks.

   (iii) Find the average power with which he is working.

2 A weightlifter takes 2 seconds to lift 120 kg from the floor to a position 2 m above it where the weight has to be held stationary.

   (i) Calculate the work done by the weightlifter.

   (ii) Calculate the average power developed by the weightlifter.

The weightlifter is using the 'clean and jerk' technique. This means that in the first stage of the lift he raises the weight 0.8 m from the floor in 0.5 s. He then holds it stationary for 1 s before lifting it up to the final position in another 0.5 s.

   (iii) Find the average power developed by the weightlifter during each of the stages of the lift.

3 A winch is used to pull a crate of mass 180 kg up a rough slope of angle $30°$ against a frictional force of 450 N. The crate moves at a steady speed, v, of $1.2 \, \text{ms}^{-1}$.

   (i) Calculate the gravitational potential energy given to the crate during 30 s.

   (ii) Calculate the work done against friction during this time.

   (iii) Calculate the total work done per second by the winch.

The cable from the winch to the crate runs parallel to the slope.

   (iv) Calculate the tension, T, in the cable.

   (v) What information is given by $T \times v$?

4 The power output from the engine of a car of mass 50 kg which is travelling along level ground at a constant speed of $33 \, \text{ms}^{-1}$ is 23 200 W.

   (i) Find the total resistance on the car under these conditions.

   (ii) You were given one piece of unnecessary information. Which is it?

5 A Kawasaki GPz 305 motorcycle has a maximum power output of 26.5 kW and a top speed of 103 mph ($46 \, \text{ms}^{-1}$). Find the force exerted by the motorcycle engine when the motorcycle is travelling at top speed.

6 A crane is raising a load of 500 tonnes at a steady rate of $5 \, \text{cm s}^{-1}$. What power is the engine of the crane producing? (Assume that there are no forces from friction or air resistance.)

7 A cyclist, travelling at a constant speed of $8 \, \text{ms}^{-1}$ along a level road, experiences a total resistance of 70 N.

   (i) Find the power which the cyclist is producing.

   (ii) Find the work done by the cyclist in 5 minutes under these conditions.

8 A conveyor belt picks up stationary sacks of grain and delivers them to a place 5 m higher with speed $1.5\,\mathrm{ms}^{-1}$. The mass of one sack is 25 kg and they are delivered at the rate of one sack every 6 s.

  (i) Calculate the total mechanical energy given to one sack by the conveyor belt.

  (ii) Calculate the average power with which the conveyor's belt is working, assuming that frictional forces may be ignored.

9 A train consists of a diesel shunter of mass 100 tonnes pulling a truck of mass 25 tonnes along a level track. The engine is working at a rate of 125 kW. The resistance to motion of the truck and shunter is 50 N per tonne.

  (i)   Calculate the constant speed of the train.

While travelling at this constant speed, the truck becomes uncoupled. The shunter engine continues to produce the same power.

  (ii)   Find the acceleration of the shunter immediately after this happens.

  (iii) Find the greatest speed the shunter can now reach.

10 A supertanker of mass $4 \times 10^8\,\mathrm{kg}$ is steaming at a constant speed of $8\,\mathrm{ms}^{-1}$. The resistance force is $2 \times 10^6\,\mathrm{N}$.

  (i)   What power are the ship's engines producing?

One of the ship's two engines suddenly fails but the other continues to work at the same rate.

  (ii)   Find the deceleration of the ship immediately after the failure.

The resistance force is directly proportional to the speed of the ship.

  (iii) Find the eventual steady speed of the ship under one engine only, assuming that the single engine maintains constant power output.

11 A car of mass 850 kg has a maximum speed of $50\,\mathrm{ms}^{-1}$ and a maximum power output of 40 kW. The resistance force, $R\,\mathrm{N}$ at speed $v\,\mathrm{ms}^{-1}$ is modelled by

$$R = kv$$

  (i)   Find the value of k.

  (ii)   Find the resistance force when the car's speed is $20\,\mathrm{ms}^{-1}$.

  (iii) Find the power needed to travel at a constant speed of $20\,\mathrm{ms}^{-1}$ along a level road.

  (iv) Find the maximum acceleration of the car when it is travelling at $20\,\mathrm{ms}^{-1}$

    (a) along a level road   **(b)** up a hill at $5°$ to the horizontal.

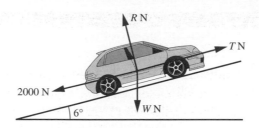

A car of mass 1 tonne is moving at a constant velocity of $60\,\mathrm{km\,h^{-1}}$ up an inclined road which makes an angle of $6°$ with the horizontal.

(i) Calculate the weight W of the car and the normal reaction R between the car and the road.

Given that the non-gravitational resistance down the slope is $2000\,\mathrm{N}$, find

(ii) the tractive force T which is propelling the car up the slope

(iii) the rate at which T is doing work.

The engine has a maximum power output of $80\,\mathrm{kW}$.

(iv) Assuming the resistances stay the same as before, calculate the maximum speed of the car up the same slope.

[MEI]

13

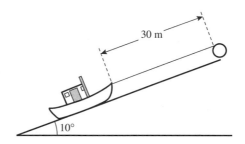

A boat of mass $1200\,\mathrm{kg}$ is winched a distance $30\,\mathrm{m}$ up a flat beach inclined at $10°$ to the horizontal.

Initially a very approximate model is used in which all resistances are neglected.

(i) Calculate the work done.

(ii) Given that the process takes 2 minutes and that the boat moves at a constant speed, calculate the power of the winch motor.

A better model takes account of the resistance of the beach to the motion. Assuming that the winch motor develops a constant $4.5\,\mathrm{kW}$, the resistance of the beach on the boat is a constant $5\,\mathrm{kN}$ and the boat moves at a constant speed,

(iii) calculate how long the winching will take

(iv) show that if the winch cable suddenly broke off at the boat whilst the winching was in progress, the boat would come to rest in about $35\,\mathrm{mm}$.

[MEI]

INVESTIGATION

CRAWLER LANES

Sometimes on single carriageway roads or even some motorways, crawler lanes are introduced for slow-moving, heavily laden lorries going uphill. Investigate how steep a slope can be before a crawler lane is needed.

Data: Typical power output for a large lorry : 45 kW

Typical mass of a large laden lorry   : 32 tonnes.

EXPERIMENT

ENERGY LOSSES

Set up a track like this one.

Figure 5.14

Release cars or trolleys from different heights and record the heights that they reach on the opposite side. Use your results to formulate a model for the force of resistance acting on them.

KEY POINTS

1 The work done by a constant force F is given by Fs where s is the distance moved in the direction of the force.

2 The kinetic energy (K.E.) of a body of mass m moving with speed v is given by $\frac{1}{2}mv^2$. Kinetic energy is the energy a body possesses on account of its motion.

3 The work–energy principle states that the total work done by all the forces acting on a body is equal to the increase in the kinetic energy of the body.

4 The gravitational potential energy of a body of mass m at height h above a given reference level is given by mgh. It is the work done against the force of gravity in raising the body.

5 Mechanical energy (K.E. and P.E.) is conserved when no forces other than gravity do work.

6 Power is the rate of doing work, and is given by Fv.

7 The S.I. unit for energy is the joule and that for power is the watt.

6 Impulse and momentum

I collided with a stationary truck coming the other way.

Statement on an insurance form reported in the Toronto News.

The karate expert in the picture has just broken a pile of roof-tiles with a single blow from his head. Forces in excess of 3000 N have been measured during karate chops. How is this possible?

Impulse

Although the karate expert produces a very large force, it acts for only a short time. This is often the case in situations where impacts occur, as in the following example involving a tennis player.

EXAMPLE 6.1

A tennis player hits the ball as it is travelling towards her at $10\,\text{ms}^{-1}$ horizontally. Immediately after she hits it, the ball is travelling away from her at $20\,\text{ms}^{-1}$ horizontally. The mass of the ball is $0.06\,\text{kg}$. What force does the tennis player apply to the ball?

SOLUTION

You cannot tell unless you know how long the impact lasts, and that will vary from one shot to another.

 Show that the average force she applies to the ball in the cases where the impact lasts 0.1 s and 0.015 s are 18 N and 120 N respectively. What does 'average' mean in this context?

While you cannot calculate the force unless you know the time for which it acts, you can work out the product force × time. This is called the *impulse*.

When a constant force acts for a time t the impulse of the force is defined as

$$\text{impulse} = \text{force} \times \text{time}.$$

The impulse is a vector in the direction of the force. When the force and time cannot be known separately, as in the case of the tennis ball, an impulse is often denoted by **J** and its magnitude by J. The S.I. unit for impulse is the newton-second (Ns).

Impulse and momentum

When the motion is in one dimension and the velocity of an object of mass m is changed from u to v by a constant force F you can use Newton's second law and the equations for motion with constant acceleration.

$$F = ma$$
and
$$v = u + at$$
$$\Rightarrow \quad mv = mu + mat$$
Substituting F for ma gives $\quad mv = mu + Ft$
$$\Rightarrow \quad Ft = mv - mu$$

The quantity 'mass × velocity' is defined as the *momentum* of the moving object.

The equation ① can then be written as

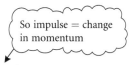

So impulse = change in momentum

$$impulse \ of \ force = final \ momentum - initial \ momentum \qquad ①$$

This equation also holds for any large force acting for a short time even when it cannot be assumed to be constant. The force on the tennis ball will increase as it embeds itself into the strings and then decrease as it is catapulted away, but you can calculate the impulse of the tennis racket on the ball as

$$0.06 \times 20 - 0.06 \times (-10) = 1.8 \, \text{Ns} \quad \text{(the −10 takes account of the change in direction)}$$

Equation ① is also true for a variable force but then calculus is used to work out the impulse. It is also true, but less often used, when a longer time is involved.

---

❷ The magnitude of the momentum of an object is often thought of as its resistance to being stopped. Compare the momentum and kinetic energy of a cricket ball of mass 0.15 kg bowled very fast at $40 \, \text{ms}^{-1}$ and a 20 tonne railway truck moving at a very slow speed of 1 cm per second.

Which would you rather be hit by, an object with high momentum and low energy, or one with high energy and low momentum?

EXAMPLE 6.2   A ball of mass 50 g hits the ground with a speed of 4 ms^{-1} and rebounds with an initial speed of 3 ms^{-1}. If the ball is in contact with the ground for 0.01 s,

(i) find the average force exerted on the ball
(ii) find the loss of kinetic energy during the impact.

SOLUTION

(i) The impulse is given by:

$$J = mv - mu$$
$$= 0.05 \times 3 - 0.05 \times (-4)$$
$$= 0.35$$

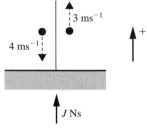

Figure 6.1

The impulse J is also given by

$$J = Ft$$

where F is the average force, i.e. the constant force which, acting for the same time interval, would have the same effect as the variable force which actually acted.

$$\therefore \qquad 0.35 = F \times 0.01$$
$$F = 35$$

So the ground exerts an average upward force of 35 N.

(ii)   Initial K.E. $= \frac{1}{2} \times 0.05 \times 4^2$
$$= 0.400 \, \text{J}$$
Final K.E. $= \frac{1}{2} \times 0.05 \times 3^2$
$$= 0.225 \, \text{J}$$
Loss in K.E. $= 0.175 \, \text{J}$

(This is converted into heat and sound.)

Note

Example 6.2 demonstrates the important point that mechanical energy is not conserved during an impact.

Although the force of gravity acts during the impact, its impulse is negligible over such a short time.

EXAMPLE 6.3

A car of mass 800 kg is pushed with a constant force of magnitude 200 N for 10 s. If the car starts from rest, find its speed at the end of the ten-second interval.

SOLUTION

The force of 200 N acts for 10 s, so the impulse on the car is

$$J = 200 \times 10 = 2000 \text{ (in Ns)}.$$
(The impulse is in the direction of the force.)

Hence the change in momentum (in Ns) is

$$mv = 2000$$
$$\therefore \qquad v = \frac{2000}{800} = 2.5$$

The speed at the end of the time interval is 2.5 ms^{-1}.

Impulse and momentum in more than one dimension

Both impulse and momentum are vectors. The impulse of a force is in the direction of the force and the momentum of a moving object is in the direction of its velocity. When an impulse **J** changes the velocity of a mass m from **u** to **v**, the impulse–momentum equation is

$$\mathbf{J} = m\mathbf{v} - m\mathbf{u}$$

The diagram shows how this applies to a ball which changes direction when it is hit by a bat.

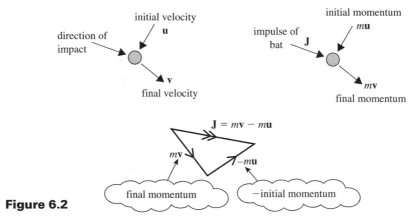

Figure 6.2

EXAMPLE 6.4

In a game of snooker the cue ball (W) of mass 0.2 kg is hit towards a stationary red ball (R) at $0.8 \, \text{ms}^{-1}$. After the collision the cue ball is moving at $0.6 \, \text{ms}^{-1}$ having been deflected through 30°.

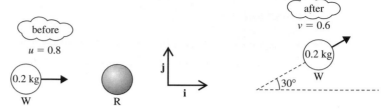

Figure 6.3

Find the impulse of the cue ball and show this in a vector diagram.

SOLUTION

In terms of unit vectors **i** and **j** the velocities before and after the collision are given by

$$\mathbf{u} = 0.8\mathbf{i}$$
$$\mathbf{v} = 0.6 \cos 30° \, \mathbf{i} + 0.6 \sin 30° \, \mathbf{j}$$

Then   impulse = final momentum − initial momentum

$$\mathbf{J} = m\mathbf{v} - m\mathbf{u}$$
$$= 0.2(0.6 \cos 30° \, \mathbf{i} + 0.6 \sin 30° \, \mathbf{j}) - 0.2(0.8\mathbf{i})$$
$$= -0.056\,\mathbf{i} + 0.06\,\mathbf{j}$$

Magnitude of impulse $= \sqrt{0.056^2 + 0.06^2}$

$$= 0.082$$

Direction: $\tan \alpha = \frac{0.06}{0.056}$

$$\alpha = 47°$$
$$\theta = 133°$$

The impulse has magnitude 0.082 N at an angle of 133° to the initial motion of the ball.

This is shown on the vector diagram below. Note that the impulse–momentum equation shows the direction of the impulsive force acting on the cue ball.

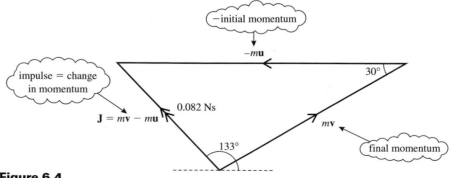

Figure 6.4

EXAMPLE 6.5

A hockey ball of mass $0.15\,\text{kg}$ is moving at $4\,\text{ms}^{-1}$ parallel to the side of a pitch when it is struck by a blow from a hockey stick that exerts an impulse of $4\,\text{Ns}$ at an angle of $120°$ to its direction of motion. Find the final velocity of the ball.

SOLUTION

The vector diagram shows the motion of the ball.

Figure 6.5

In terms of unit vectors $\mathbf{i}$ and $\mathbf{j}$ we have

$$\mathbf{u} = 4\mathbf{i}$$

and
$$\mathbf{J} = -4\cos 60°\,\mathbf{i} + 4\sin 60°\,\mathbf{j}$$
$$= -2\mathbf{i} + 3.46\mathbf{j}$$

Using
$$\mathbf{J} = m\mathbf{v} - m\mathbf{u}$$
$$-2\mathbf{i} + 3.46\mathbf{j} = 0.15\mathbf{v} - 0.15 \times 4\mathbf{i}$$
$$\Rightarrow \qquad 0.15\mathbf{v} = -2\mathbf{i} + 0.6\mathbf{i} + 3.46\mathbf{j}$$
$$\Rightarrow \qquad 0.15\mathbf{v} = -1.4\mathbf{i} + 3.46\mathbf{j}$$
$$\Rightarrow \qquad \mathbf{v} = -9.33\mathbf{i} + 23.1\mathbf{j}$$

The magnitude of the velocity is given by $v = \sqrt{9.33^2 + 23.1^2}$
$$= 24.9\ \text{ms}^{-1}$$

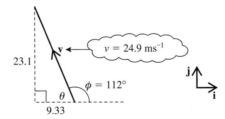

Figure 6.6

The angle, θ, is given by $\theta = \tan^{-1}\left(\frac{23.1}{9.33}\right)$

$$= 68°$$
$$\phi = 180° - 68°$$
$$= 112°.$$

After the blow, the ball has a velocity of magnitude $24.9\,\text{ms}^{-1}$ at an angle of $112°$ to the original direction of motion.

The motion of a particle under a variable force

Very often the forces that change the motion of objects are not constant. When a trampolinist hits the bed of a trampoline, the upward force acting on her is linked to the deformation of the bed and the extension of the springs.

The greater the deformation and extension, the greater the force. While it is possible to deal with situations like this by considering the average force, it is also possible to deal precisely with variable forces.

Motion under a variable force is also covered by the impulse–momentum equation. Think of a particle of mass m moving along a straight line and subject to a variable force F for a time T.

Suppose that during this time the velocity of the particle changes from U to V.

Applying Newton's second law

$$F = ma = m\frac{\mathrm{d}v}{\mathrm{d}t}$$

Integrating between $t = 0$ and $t = T$ we have

$$\int_0^T F\,\mathrm{d}t = \int_0^T m\frac{\mathrm{d}v}{\mathrm{d}t}\,\mathrm{d}t$$
$$= \int_{v=U}^{v=V} m\,\mathrm{d}v$$
$$= mV - mU$$

> Change the limits:
> when $t = 0$, $v = U$
> when $t = T$, $v = V$

The right-hand side of the equation is the change in momentum and the left-hand side, $\int_0^T F\,\mathrm{d}t$, is the impulse. The impulse is therefore the area under the graph of F against t.

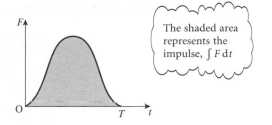

Figure 6.7

Note that if the force, F, is constant then

$$\text{impulse} = \int_0^T F\,dt = F\int_0^T dt = FT \text{ as before.}$$

1 Find the momentum of the following objects, assuming each of them to be travelling in a straight line.
   (i)   An ice skater of mass 50 kg travelling with speed $10\,\text{ms}^{-1}$.
   (ii) An elephant of mass 5 tonnes moving at $4\,\text{ms}^{-1}$.
   (iii) A train of mass 7000 tonnes travelling at $40\,\text{ms}^{-1}$.
   (iv) A bacterium of mass $2 \times 10^{-16}\,\text{g}$ moving with speed $1\,\text{mm s}^{-1}$.

2 Calculate the impulse required in each of these situations:
   (i)   to stop a car of mass 1.3 tonnes travelling at $14\,\text{ms}^{-1}$
   (ii) to putt a golf ball of mass 1.5 g with speed $1.5\,\text{ms}^{-1}$
   (iii) to stop a cricket ball of mass 0.15 kg travelling at $20\,\text{ms}^{-1}$
   (iv) to fire a bullet of mass 25 g with speed $400\,\text{ms}^{-1}$.

3 A stone of mass 1.5 kg is dropped from rest. After a time interval t s, it has fallen a distance s m and has velocity $v\,\text{ms}^{-1}$.

   Take g to be $10\,\text{ms}^{-2}$ and neglect air resistance.
   (i)   Write down the force F (in N) acting on the stone.
   (ii) Find the distance, s, that the stone has fallen when $t = 2$.
   (iii) Find the velocity, v (in ms^{-1}) of the stone when $t = 2$.
   (iv) Write down the value, units and meaning of Fs and explain why this has the same value as $\frac{1}{2} \times 1.5v^2$.
   (v)   Write down the value, units and meaning of Ft and explain why this has the same value as $1.5v$.

4 A girl throws a ball of mass 0.06 kg vertically upwards with initial speed $20\,\text{ms}^{-1}$.

   Take g to be $10\,\text{ms}^{-2}$ and neglect air resistance.
   (i)   What is the initial momentum of the ball?
   (ii) How long does it take for the ball to reach the top of its flight?
   (iii) What is the momentum of the ball when it is at the top of its flight?
   (iv) What impulse acted on the ball over the period between its being thrown and its reaching maximum height?

5 A netball of mass 425 g is moving horizontally with speed 5 ms^{-1} when it is caught.

  (i) Find the impulse needed to stop the ball.

  (ii) Find the average force needed to stop the ball if it takes

   (a) 0.1 s   **(b)** 0.05 s.

  (iii) Why does the action of taking a ball into your body make it easier to catch?

6 A car of mass 0.9 tonnes is travelling at 13.2 ms^{-1} when it crashes head-on into a wall. The car is brought to rest in a time of 0.12 s. Find

  (i) the impulse acting on the car

  (ii) the average force acting on the car

  (iii) the average deceleration of the car in terms of g (taken to be 10 ms^{-2}).

  (iv) Explain why many cars are designed with crumple zones rather than with completely rigid construction.

7 Boris is sleeping on a bunk-bed at a height of 1.5 m when he rolls over and falls out. His mass is 20 kg.

  (i) Find the speed with which he hits the floor.

  (ii) Find the impulse that the floor has exerted on him when he has come to rest.

  (iii) Find the impulse he has exerted on the floor.

  It takes Boris 0.2 s to come to rest.

  (iv) Find the average force acting on him during this time.

8 A railway truck of mass 10 tonnes is travelling at 3 ms^{-1} along a siding when it hits some buffers. After the impact it is travelling at 1.5 ms^{-1} in the opposite direction.

  (i) Find the initial momentum of the truck, remembering to specify its direction.

  (ii) Find the momentum of the truck after it has left the buffers.

  (iii) Find the impulse that has acted on the truck.

  During the impact the force F N that the buffers exert on the truck varies as shown in this graph.

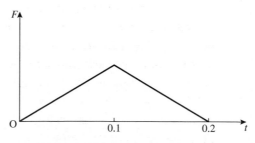

  (iv) State what information is given by the area under the graph.

  (v) What is the greatest value of the force F?

9 A snooker ball of mass 0.08 kg is travelling with speed 3.5 ms⁻¹ when it hits the cushion at an angle of 60°. After the impact the ball is travelling with speed 2 ms⁻¹ at an angle 30° to the cushion.

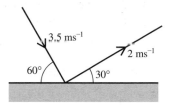

(i) Draw accurate scale diagrams to represent the following vectors:
   (a) the momentum of the ball before impact
   (b) the momentum of the ball after impact
   (c) the change in momentum of the ball during impact.

(ii) Use your answer to part (i) (c) to *estimate* the magnitude and direction of the impulse acting on the ball.

(iii) Resolve the velocity of the ball before and after impact into components parallel and perpendicular to the cushion.

(iv) Use your answers to part (iii) to *calculate* the impulse which acts on the ball during its impact with the cushion. Comment on your answers.

10 A hockey ball of mass 0.15 kg is travelling with velocity $12\mathbf{i} - 8\mathbf{j}$ (in ms⁻¹), where the unit vectors $\mathbf{i}$ and $\mathbf{j}$ are in horizontal directions parallel and perpendicular to the length of the pitch, and the vector $\mathbf{k}$ is vertically upwards. The ball is hit by Jane with an impulse $-4.8\mathbf{i} + 1.2\mathbf{j}$.

(i) What is the velocity of the ball immediately after Jane has hit it?

The ball goes straight, without losing any speed, to Fatima in the opposite team who hits it without stopping it. Its velocity is now $14\mathbf{i} + 4\mathbf{j} + 3\mathbf{k}$.

(ii) What impulse does Fatima give the ball?

(iii) Which player hits the ball harder?

11 A hailstone of mass 4 g is travelling with speed 20 ms⁻¹ when it hits a window as shown in the diagram. It bounces off the window; the vertical component of the velocity is unaltered, but the horizontal component is now 2 ms⁻¹ away from the window.

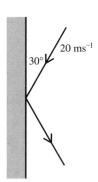

(i) State the magnitude and direction of the impulse
   (a) of the window on the hailstone
   (b) of the hailstone on the window.

At the peak of the storm, hailstones like this are hitting the window at the rate of 540 per minute.

(ii) Find the average force of the hail on the window.

12 The graph shows the magnitude of the driving force on a van during the first 4 s after it starts from rest. The mass of the van is 2500 kg.

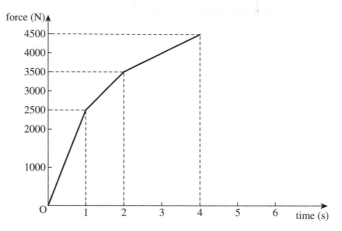

(i)   What information is given by the area under the graph?
(ii) Find the total impulse on the van over the whole interval.
(iii) Find the final speed of the van, ignoring the effect of air resistance.

Conservation of momentum

Collisions

In an experiment to investigate car design two vehicles were made to collide head-on. How would you investigate this situation? Can you find a relationship between the change in momentum of the van and that of the car?

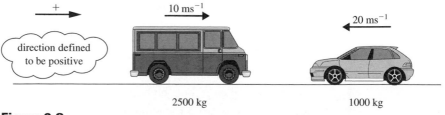

Figure 6.8

The first thing to remember is Newton's third law. The force that body A exerts on body B is equal to the force that B exerts on A, but in the opposite direction.

Suppose that once the van is in contact with the car, it exerts a force F on the car for a time t. Newton's third law tells us that the car also exerts a force F on the van for a time t. (This applies whether F is constant or variable.) So both vehicles receive equal impulses, but in opposite directions. Consequently the increase in momentum of the car in the positive direction is exactly equal to the increase in momentum of the van in the negative direction. For the two vehicles together, the total change in momentum is zero.

This example illustrates the *law of conservation of momentum*.

> *The law of conservation of momentum states that when there are no external influences on a system, the total momentum of the system is constant.*

Since momentum is a vector quantity, this applies to the magnitude of the momentum in any direction.

For a collision, you can say

total momentum before collision = total momentum after collision

 It is important to remember that although momentum is conserved in a collision, mechanical energy is not conserved. Some of the work done by the forces is converted into heat and sound.

EXAMPLE 6.6

The two vehicles in the previous discussion collide head-on, and as a result the van comes to rest.

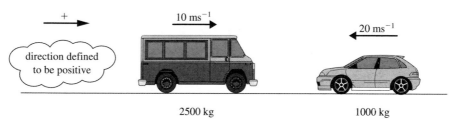

Figure 6.9

Find

(i) the final velocity of the car, $v\,\text{ms}^{-1}$
(ii) the impulse on each vehicle
(iii) the kinetic energy lost.
(iv) If it is assumed that the impact lasts for one-twentieth of a second, find the force on each vehicle and its acceleration.

SOLUTION

(i)

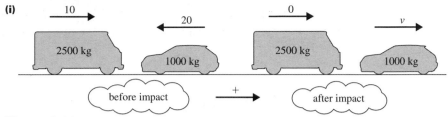

Figure 6.10

Using conservation of momentum, and taking the positive direction as being to the right:

$$2500 \times 10 + 1000 \times (-20) = 2500 \times 0 + 1000 \times v$$
$$5000 = 1000v$$
$$v = 5$$

The final velocity of the car is $5\,\text{ms}^{-1}$ in the positive direction (i.e. the car travels backwards).

(ii)   Impulse = final momentum − initial momentum

For the van,   impulse $= 2500 \times 0 - 2500 \times 10$
$$= -25\,000\,\text{Ns}.$$

For the car,   impulse $= 1000 \times 5 - 1000 \times (-20)$
$$= +25\,000\,\text{Ns}.$$

The van experiences an impulse of $25\,000\,\text{Ns}$ in the negative direction, the car an equal and opposite impulse.

(iii)   Total initial K.E. $= \frac{1}{2} \times 2500 \times 10^2 + \frac{1}{2} \times 1000 \times 20^2$
$$= 325\,000\,\text{J}$$

Total final K.E. $= \frac{1}{2} \times 2500 \times 0^2 + \frac{1}{2} \times 1000 \times 5^2$
$$= 12\,500\,\text{J}$$

Loss in K.E. $= 312\,500\,\text{J}$

(iv)   Impulse = average force × time
$$25\,000 = F \times \tfrac{1}{20}$$
$$F = 500\,000\,\text{N (acting to the right on the car}$$
$$\text{and to the left on the van).}$$

Using $F = ma$ on each vehicle gives an average acceleration of $500\,\text{ms}^{-2}$ for the car and $-200\,\text{ms}^{-2}$ for the van.

❓ These accelerations ($500\,\text{ms}^{-2}$ and $-200\,\text{ms}^{-2}$) seem very high. Are they realistic for a head-on collision?

Work out the distance each car travels during the time interval of one-twentieth of a second between impact and separation. This will give you an idea of the amount of damage there would be.

Is it better for cars to be made strong so that there is little damage, or to be designed to crumple under impact?

Set up the apparatus as shown in figure 6.11. Truck A can be released from the top of the slope so that it always hits truck B at the same speed.

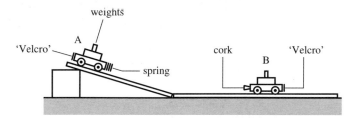

Figure 6.11

For each situation below describe what you think will happen and then test your prediction.

1 Arrange the trucks so that the spring on truck A hits the cork on truck B.
   (i) Load both trucks with the same mass, then release A so that it rolls down and hits B.
   (ii) Now load B so that it is very much heavier than A.
   (iii) Now load A so that it is very much heavier than B.
2 Arrange the trucks so that the velcro tabs hit each other during the collision. Now repeat experiments (i) to (iii) above.
3 Rearrange the track as shown below.

Figure 6.12

   (i) Release trucks that are loaded equally from both ends of the track, so that the spring and cork come into contact.
   (ii) Repeat (i), but with one truck loaded so that it is much heavier than the other.
   (iii) Release equally loaded trucks from each end so that the velcro ends come into contact.
   (iv) Repeat (iii), but with one truck loaded so that it is much heavier than the other.

EXAMPLE 6.7

In an experiment on lorry bumper design, the Transport Research Laboratory arranged for a car and a lorry, of masses 1 and 3.5 tonnes to travel towards each other, both with speed $9\,\text{ms}^{-1}$. After colliding both vehicles moved together and the total momentum had been conserved.

What was their combined velocity after the collision?

SOLUTION

The situation before the collision is illustrated below.

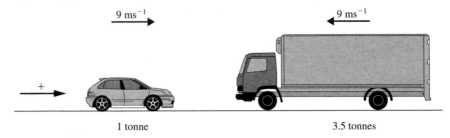

Figure 6.13

Taking the positive direction to be to the right, before the collision

momentum of the car in Ns: $1000 \times 9 = 9000$

momentum of the lorry in Ns: $3500 \times (-9) = -31\,500$

total momentum in Ns: $9000 - 31\,500 = -22\,500$

After the collision assume they move as a single object of mass 4.5 tonnes with velocity $v\,\text{ms}^{-1}$ in the positive direction so the total momentum is now $4500v\,\text{Ns}$.

Momentum is conserved so $4500v = -22\,500$

$$v = -5$$

The car and lorry move at $5\,\text{ms}^{-1}$ in the direction the lorry was moving.

EXAMPLE 6.8

A child of mass 30 kg running through a supermarket at $4\,\text{ms}^{-1}$ leaps on to a stationary shopping trolley of mass 15 kg. Find the speed of the child and trolley together, assuming that the trolley is free to move easily.

SOLUTION

The diagram shows the situation before the child hits the trolley.

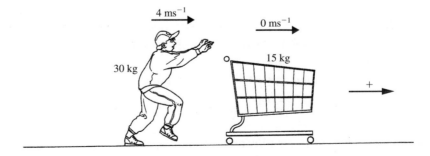

Figure 6.14

Taking the direction of the child's velocity as positive, total momentum (in Ns) before impact

$$= 4 \times 30 + 0 \times 15$$
$$= 120.$$

The situation after impact is shown below.

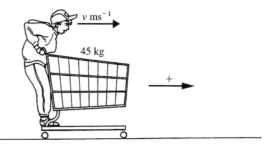

Figure 6.15

The total mass of child and trolley is 45 kg, so the total momentum after is $45v$ Ns.

Conservation of momentum gives:

$$45v = 120$$
$$v = 2\tfrac{2}{3}.$$

The child and the trolley together move at $2\tfrac{2}{3}$ ms^{-1}.

Explosions

Conservation of momentum also applies when explosions take place provided there are no external forces. For example when a bullet is fired from a rifle, or a rocket is launched.

EXAMPLE 6.9

A rifle of mass 8 kg is used to fire a bullet of mass 80 g at a speed of 200 ms^{-1}. Calculate the initial recoil speed of the rifle.

SOLUTION

Before the bullet is fired the total momentum of the system is zero.

Before firing: rifle and bullet have zero momentum

Figure 6.16

After the firing the situation is as illustrated below.

Figure 6.17

The total momentum in the positive direction after the firing is
$8v + 0.08 \times 200$.

For momentum to be conserved,

$$8v + 0.08 \times 200 = 0$$

so that

$$8v = -200 \times 0.08$$

$$v = -2$$

> You have probably realised that v would turn out to be negative

The recoil speed of the rifle is $2\,\text{ms}^{-1}$.

EXERCISE 6B

1 A spaceship of mass 50 000 kg travelling with speed $200\,\text{ms}^{-1}$ docks with a space station of mass 500 000 kg travelling in the same direction with speed $195\,\text{ms}^{-1}$. What is their speed after the docking is completed?

2 A railway truck of mass 20 tonnes is shunted with speed $3\,\text{ms}^{-1}$ towards a stationary truck of mass 10 tonnes. What is its speed after impact
   (i) if it remains in contact with the second truck
   (ii) if the second truck now moves at $3\,\text{ms}^{-1}$?

3 The driver of a car of mass 1000 kg falls asleep while it is travelling at $30\,\text{ms}^{-1}$. The car runs into the back of the car in front which has mass 800 kg and is travelling in the same direction at $20\,\text{ms}^{-1}$. The bumpers of the two cars become locked together and they continue as one vehicle.
   (i) What is the final speed of the cars?
   (ii) What impulse does the larger car give to the smaller one?
   (iii) What impulse does the smaller car give to the larger one?

4 A lorry of mass 5 tonnes is towing a car of mass 1 tonne. Initially the tow rope is slack and the car stationary. As the rope becomes taut the lorry is travelling at $2\,\text{ms}^{-1}$.
   (i) Find the speed of the car once it is being towed.
   (ii) Find the magnitude of the impulse transmitted by the tow rope and state the direction of the impulse on each vehicle.

5 A bullet of mass 50 g is moving horizontally at $200\,\mathrm{ms}^{-1}$ when it becomes embedded in a stationary block of mass 16 kg which is free to slide on a smooth horizontal table.

(i) Calculate the speed of the bullet and the block after the impact.

(ii) Find the impulse from the bullet on the block.

The bullet takes 0.01 s to come to rest relative to the block.

(iii) What is the average force acting on the bullet while it is decelerating?

6 A spaceship of mass 50 000 kg is travelling through space with speed $5000\,\mathrm{ms}^{-1}$ when a crew member throws a box of mass 5 kg out of the back with speed $10\,\mathrm{ms}^{-1}$ relative to the spaceship.

(i) What is the absolute speed of the box?

(ii) What is the speed of the spaceship after the box has been thrown out?

7 A gun of mass 500 kg fires a shell of mass 5 kg horizontally with muzzle speed $300\,\mathrm{ms}^{-1}$.

(i) Calculate the recoil speed of the gun.

An army commander would like soldiers to be able to fire such a shell from a rifle held against their shoulders (so they can attack armoured vehicles).

(ii) Explain why such an idea has no hope of success.

8 Manoj (mass 70 kg) and Alka (mass 50 kg) are standing stationary facing each other on a smooth ice rink. They then push against each other with a force of 35 N for 1.5 s. The direction in which Manoj faces is taken as positive.

(i) What is their total momentum before they start pushing?

(ii) Find the velocity of each of them after they have finished pushing.

(iii) Find the momentum of each of them after they have finished pushing.

(iv) What is their total momentum after they have finished pushing?

9 Katherine (mass 40 kg) and Elisabeth (mass 30 kg) are on a sledge (mass 10 kg) which is travelling across smooth horizontal ice at $5\,\mathrm{ms}^{-1}$. Katherine jumps off the back of the sledge with speed $4\,\mathrm{ms}^{-1}$ backwards relative to the sledge.

(i) What is Katherine's absolute speed when she jumps off?

(ii) With what speed does Elisabeth, still on the sledge, then go?

Elisabeth then jumps off in the same manner, also with speed $4\,\mathrm{ms}^{-1}$ relative to the sledge.

(iii) What is the speed of the sledge now?

(iv) What would the final speed of the sledge have been if Katherine and Elisabeth had both jumped off at the same time, with speed $4\,\mathrm{ms}^{-1}$ backwards relative to the sledge?

10 A truck P of mass 2000 kg starts from rest and moves down an incline from A to B as illustrated in the diagram. The distance from A to B is 50 m and $\sin \alpha = 0.05$. CBDE is horizontal.

Neglecting resistance to motion, calculate
(i) the potential energy lost by the truck P as it moves from A to B
(ii) the speed of the truck P at B.

Truck P then continues from B without loss of speed towards a second truck Q of mass 1500 kg at rest at D. The two trucks collide and move on towards E together. Still neglecting resistances to motion, calculate
(iii) the common speed of the two trucks just after they become coupled together
(iv) the percentage loss of kinetic energy in the collision.

[MEI]

11 A pile-driver has a block of mass 2 tonnes which is dropped from a height of 5 m on to a pile of mass 600 kg which it is driving vertically into the ground. The block rebounds with a speed of 2 ms^{-1} immediately after the impact. Taking g to be 10 ms^{-2} find
(i) the speed of the block immediately before the impact
(ii) the impulse acting on the block
(iii) the impulse acting on the pile.

From the moment of impact the pile takes 0.025 s to come to rest.
(iv) Calculate the force of resistance on the pile, assuming it to be constant.
(v) How far does the pile move?

12 A one-tonne spacecraft which is travelling at a speed of 9500 ms^{-1} is hit by a piece of debris of mass 0.5 kg travelling at right angles to it at the same speed. As a result of the impact, the debris melts into the wall of the spacecraft leaving a 12 cm hole. Estimate
(i) the velocity of the spacecraft after the crash
(ii) the total kinetic energy lost by the debris during the impact
(iii) the average force acting during the impact.

13 A sledge of mass 5 kg is initially at rest on a smooth, horizontal surface. All resistances to motion may be neglected. Give all answers correct to three significant figures.
(i) A snowball of mass 0.1 kg is thrown at the sledge, strikes it horizontally at 10 ms^{-1} and coalesces with it. At what speed does the sledge move off?
(ii) If a second identical snowball is thrown in the same way, what will the new speed of the sledge be?
(iii) After n identical snowballs have been thrown in the same way show that the speed of the sledge, v ms^{-1} is given by $v = \dfrac{n}{5 + 0.1n}$.

(iv) Show that the expression in (iii) may be written as $v = 10 - \dfrac{50}{5 + 0.1n}$ and hence sketch a graph of the relationship between v and n. How does the velocity of the sledge change as n increases?

(v) If the snowball were replaced by a rubber ball of the same mass as in (i), so that it bounced back off the sledge, would the speed of the sledge be greater, the same or less? Give brief reasons for your answer.

[MEI]

14 Ben, whose mass is 80 kg, is standing at the front of a sleigh of length 5 m and mass 40 kg. The sleigh is initially stationary and on smooth ice. Ben then walks towards the back with speed 1 ms^{-1} relative to the sleigh.

(i) Find the velocity of the sleigh while Ben is walking towards the back of it.

(ii) Show that, throughout his walk, the combined centre of mass of Ben and the sleigh does not move.

(iii) Investigate whether the result in part (ii) is true in general for this type of situation, or is just a fluke depending on the particular values given to the variables involved.

Newton's law of impact

 If you drop two different balls, say a tennis ball and a cricket ball, from the same height, will they both rebound to the same height? How will the heights of the second bounces compare with the heights of the first ones?

Your own experience probably tells you that different balls will rebound to different heights. For example, a tennis ball will rebound to a greater height than a cricket ball. Furthermore, the surface on which the ball is dropped will affect the bounce. A tennis ball dropped onto a concrete floor will rebound higher than if dropped onto a carpeted floor. The following experiment allows you to look at this situation more closely.

EXPERIMENT

The aim of this experiment is to investigate what happens when balls bounce. Make out a table to record your results.

1 Drop a ball from a variety of heights and record the heights of release h_a and rebound h_s. Repeat several times for each height.

2 Use your values of h_a and h_s, to calculate v_a and v_s, the speeds on impact and rebound. Enter the results in your table.

3 Calculate the ratio $\dfrac{v_a}{v_s}$ for each pair of readings of h_a and h_s and enter the results in your table.

4 What do you notice about these ratios?

5 Repeat the experiment with different types of ball.

Coefficient of restitution

Newton's experiments on collisions led him to formulate a simple law relating to the speeds before and after a direct collision between two bodies, called *Newton's law of impact.*

●
$$\frac{\text{speed of separation}}{\text{speed of approach}} = \text{constant}$$

This can also be written as

$$\text{speed of separation} = \text{constant} \times \text{speed of approach}$$

This constant is called the *coefficient of restitution* and is conventionally denoted by the letter e. For two particular surfaces, e is a constant between 0 and 1. It does not have units, being the ratio of two speeds.

For very bouncy balls, e is close to 1, and for balls that do not bounce, e is close to 0. A collision for which $e = 1$ is called perfectly elastic, and a collision for which $e = 0$ is called perfectly inelastic.

Direct impact with a fixed surface

The value of e for the ball that you used in the experiment is given by $\frac{v_s}{v_a}$, and you should have found that this had approximately the same value each time for any particular ball.

When a moving object hits a fixed surface which is perpendicular to its motion it rebounds in the opposite direction. If the speed of approach is v_a and the speed of separation is v_s Newton's law of impact gives

$$\frac{v_s}{v_a} = e$$

$$\Rightarrow \quad v_s = ev_a$$

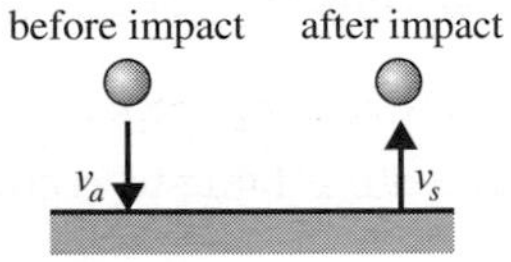

before impact   after impact

v_a ↓ v_s ↑

Figure 6.18

Collisions between bodies moving in the same straight line

Figure 6.19 shows two objects that collide while moving along a straight line. Object A is catching up with B, and after the collision either B moves away from A or they continue together.

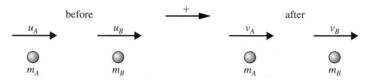

Figure 6.19

Speed of approach: $u_A - u_B$. $u_A > u_B$ for the collision to occur

Speed of separation: $v_B - v_A$. $v_B > v_A$ as B moves away from A

By Newton's law

$$\text{speed of separation} = e \times \text{speed of approach}$$
$$\Rightarrow \qquad v_B - v_A = e(u_A - u_B) \qquad ①$$

A second equation relating the velocities follows from the law of conservation of momentum in the positive direction ($\rightarrow$):

$$\text{momentum after collision} = \text{momentum before collision}$$
$$m_A v_A + m_B v_B = m_A u_A + m_B u_B \qquad ②$$

These two equations, ① and ②, allow you to calculate the final velocities, v_A and v_B, after any collision as shown in the next two examples.

EXAMPLE 6.10

A direct collision takes place between two snooker balls. The cue ball travelling at $2\,\text{ms}^{-1}$ hits a stationary red ball. After the collision the red ball moves in the direction in which the cue ball was moving before the collision. Assume that the balls have equal mass, and that the coefficient of restitution between the two balls is 0.6. Predict the velocities of the two balls after the collision.

SOLUTION

Let the mass of each ball be m, and call the (white) cue ball 'W' and the red ball 'R'. The situation is summarised in figure 6.20.

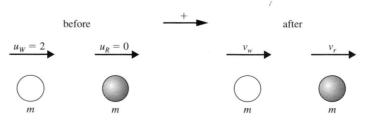

Figure 6.20

$$\text{Speed of approach} = 2 - 0 = 2$$
$$\text{Speed of separation} = v_R - v_W$$

By Newton's law of impact,

$$\text{speed of separation} = e \times \text{speed of approach}$$
$$\Rightarrow \qquad v_R - v_W = 0.6 \times 2$$
$$\Rightarrow \qquad v_R - v_W = 1.2. \qquad\qquad ①$$

Conservation of momentum gives

$$mv_W + mv_R = mu_W + mu_R$$

Dividing through by m, and substituting $u_W = 2$, $u_R = 0$, this becomes

$$v_W + v_R = 2 \qquad\qquad ②$$

Adding equations ① and ② gives $2v_R = 3.2$,

so $v_R = 1.6$, and from equation ②, $v_W = 0.4$.

After the collision both balls move forward, the red ball at a speed of $1.6\,\text{ms}^{-1}$ and the cue ball at a speed of $0.4\,\text{ms}^{-1}$.

EXAMPLE 6.11

An object A of mass m moving with speed $2u$ hits an object B of mass $2m$ moving with speed u in the opposite direction from A.

(i) Show that the ratio of speeds remains unchanged whatever the value of e.

(ii) Find the loss of kinetic energy in terms of m, u and e.

SOLUTION

(i) Let the velocities of A and B after the collision be v_A and v_B respectively.

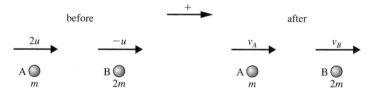

Figure 6.21

$$\text{Speed of approach} = 2u - (-u) = 3u$$
$$\text{Speed of separation} = v_B - v_A$$

Using Newton's law of impact

$$\text{speed of separation} = e \times \text{speed of approach}$$
$$\Rightarrow \qquad v_B - v_A = e \times 3u \qquad\qquad ①$$

Conservation of momentum gives

$$mv_A + 2mv_B = m(2u) + 2m(-u)$$

Dividing by m gives

$$v_A + 2v_B = 0 \qquad \textcircled{2}$$

Equation $\textcircled{1}$ is $\qquad v_B - v_A = 3eu$

Adding $\textcircled{1}$ and $\textcircled{2}$ $\qquad 3v_B = 3eu$

$$v_B = eu$$

From $\textcircled{2}$, $\qquad v_A = -2eu$

The ratio of speeds was initially $2u : u$ and finally $2eu : eu$
so the ratio of speeds is unchanged at $2 : 1$ (providing $e \neq 0$).

(ii) Initial K.E. of A $\qquad \frac{1}{2}m \times (2u)^2 = 2mu^2$

Initial K.E. of B $\qquad \frac{1}{2}(2m) \times u^2 = mu^2$

Total K.E. before impact $\qquad = 3mu^2$.

Final K.E. of A $\qquad \frac{1}{2}m \times 4e^2u^2 = 2me^2u^2$

Final K.E. of B $\qquad \frac{1}{2}(2m) \times e^2u^2 = me^2u^2$

Total K.E. after impact $\qquad = 3me^2u^2$

Loss of K.E. $\qquad = 3mu^2(1 - e^2)$.

Note

In this case, A and B lose *all* their energy when $e = 0$, but this is not true in general. Only when $e = 1$ is there *no* loss in K.E. Kinetic energy is lost in any collision in which the coefficient of restitution is not equal to 1.

You will find it helpful to draw diagrams when answering these questions.

1 In each of the situations shown below, find the unknown quantity, either the initial speed u, the final speed v or the coefficient of restitution e.

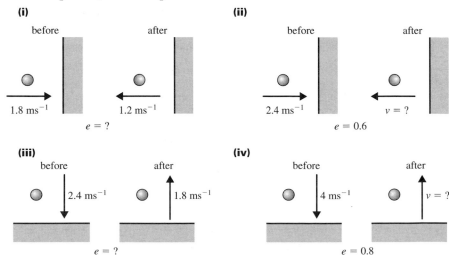

(i)

before   after

1.8 ms^{-1} 1.2 ms^{-1}

$e = ?$

(ii)

before   after

2.4 ms^{-1} $v = ?$

$e = 0.6$

(iii)

before   after

2.4 ms^{-1} 1.8 ms^{-1}

$e = ?$

(iv)

before   after

4 ms^{-1} $v = ?$

$e = 0.8$

2 Find the coefficient of restitution in the following situations.
  (i) A football hits the goalpost at $10\,\text{ms}^{-1}$ and rebounds in the opposite direction with speed $3\,\text{ms}^{-1}$.
  (ii) A beanbag is thrown against the wall with speed $5\,\text{ms}^{-1}$ and falls straight down to the ground.
  (iii) A superball is dropped onto the ground, landing with speed $8\,\text{ms}^{-1}$ and rebounding with speed $7.6\,\text{ms}^{-1}$.
  (iv) A photon approaches a mirror along a line normal to its surface with speed $3 \times 10^8\,\text{ms}^{-1}$ and leaves it along the same line with speed $3 \times 10^8\,\text{ms}^{-1}$.

3 A tennis ball of mass 60 g is hit against a practice wall. At the moment of impact it is travelling horizontally with speed $15\,\text{ms}^{-1}$. Just after the impact its speed is $12\,\text{ms}^{-1}$, also horizontally. Find
  (i) the coefficient of restitution between the ball and the wall
  (ii) the impulse acting on the ball
  (iii) the loss of kinetic energy during the impact.

4 A ball of mass 80 g is dropped from a height of 1 m on to a level floor and bounces back to a height of 0.81 m. Find
  (i) the speed of the ball just before it hits the floor
  (ii) the speed of the ball just after it has hit the floor
  (iii) the coefficient of restitution
  (iv) the change in the kinetic energy of the ball from just before it hits the floor to just after it leaves the floor
  (v) the change in the potential energy of the ball from the moment when it was dropped to the moment when it reaches the top of its first bounce
  (vi) the height of the ball's next bounce.

5 Two children drive dodgems straight at each other, and collide head-on. Both dodgems have the same mass (including their drivers) of 150 kg. Isobel is driving at $3\,\text{ms}^{-1}$, Stuart at $2\,\text{ms}^{-1}$. After the collision Isobel is stationary. Find
  (i) Stuart's velocity after the collision
  (ii) the coefficient of restitution between the cars
  (iii) the impulse acting on Stuart's car
  (iv) the kinetic energy lost in the collision.

6 A trapeze artist of mass 50 kg falls from a height of 20 m into a safety net.
  (i) Find the speed with which she hits the net. (You may ignore air resistance and should take the value of g to be $10\,\text{ms}^{-2}$.)

  Her speed on leaving the net is $15\,\text{ms}^{-1}$.
  (ii) What is the coefficient of restitution between her and the net?
  (iii) What impulse does the trapeze artist receive?
  (iv) How much mechanical energy is absorbed in the impact?
  (v) If you were a trapeze artist would you prefer a safety net with a high coefficient of restitution or a low one?

7 In each of the situations (a)–(f), a collision is about to occur. Masses are given in kilograms, speeds are in metres per second.

   (i)   Draw diagrams showing the situations before and after the impact, indicating the values of any velocities which you know, and the symbols you are using for those which you do not know.

   (ii) Use the equations corresponding to the law of conservation of momentum and to Newton's law of impact to find the final velocities.

   (iii) Find the loss of kinetic energy during the collision.

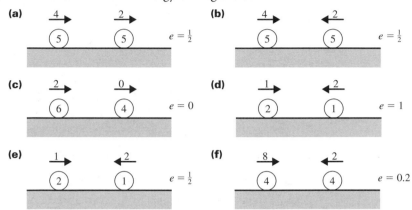

8 Two spheres of equal mass, m, are travelling towards each other along the same straight line when they collide. Both have speed v just before the collision and the coefficient of restitution between them is e. Your answers should be given in terms of m, v and e.

   (i)   Draw diagrams to show the situation before and after the collision.

   (ii) Find the velocities of the spheres after the collision.

   (iii) Show that the kinetic energy lost in the collision is given by $mv^2(1-e^2)$.

   (iv) Use the result in part (iii) to show that e cannot have a value greater than 1.

9 Three identical spheres are lying in the same straight line. The coefficient of restitution between any pair of spheres is $\frac{1}{2}$. The left-hand ball is given speed $2\,\text{ms}^{-1}$ towards the other two. What are the final velocities of all three, when no more collisions can occur?

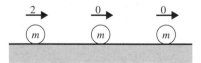

10 The diagram shows two snooker balls and one edge cushion. The coefficient of restitution between the balls and the cushion is 0.5 and that between the balls is 0.75. Ball A (the cue ball) is hit directly towards the stationary ball B with speed $8\,\text{ms}^{-1}$. Find the speeds and directions of the two balls after their second impact with each other.

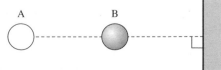

11 A sphere, A, of mass 40 g travels with speed 3 ms^{-1} along the line of centres towards another sphere, B, of the same size but of mass 60 g which is initially stationary. After the collision sphere A is stationary.

    (i) Draw diagrams to illustrate the situation before and after the collision.

    (ii) Find the velocity of sphere B after the collision.

    (iii) Find the coefficient of restitution between the spheres.

This situation may be generalised so that sphere A, of mass m_1, moving with speed u_1 along the line of centres collide with the stationary sphere B, of mass m_2. After the collision sphere A is stationary. The coefficient of restitution between the spheres is e.

    (iv) Show that $e = \dfrac{m_1}{m_2}$

    (v) What does this tell you about the relative mass of the two spheres?

    (vi) Find the ratio of the kinetic energy after impact to that before impact and write it in terms of e. What must be the value of e if kinetic energy is to be conserved when the spheres collide?

12 The coefficient of restitution between a ball and the floor is e. The ball is dropped from a height h. Air resistance may be neglected, and your answers should be given in terms of e, h, g and n, the number of bounces.

    (i) Find the time it takes the ball to reach the ground and its speed when it arrives there.

    (ii) Find the ball's height at the top of its first bounce.

    (iii) Find the height of the ball at the top of its nth bounce.

    (iv) Find the time that has elapsed when the ball hits the ground for the second time, and for the nth time.

    (v) Show that according to this model the ball comes to rest within a finite time having completed an infinite number of bounces.

    (vi) What distance does the ball travel before coming to rest?

13 A number of identical balls are free to move along a straight line on a smooth, horizontal table. In all collisions $e = 1$.

    (i) One ball A with speed u collides directly with a ball B at rest. Show that ball A is brought to rest and ball B moves off with speed u.

    (ii) Two balls B and C are placed close together at rest. Ball A is projected towards ball B at speed u. Describe the subsequent motion. (Draw a clear diagram showing velocities.)

    (iii) Two further balls D and E are added to the line in (ii) and A is projected as before. What will happen in this case?

    (iv)

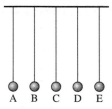

A version of 'Newton's Cradle' comprises five balls of equal size and mass hanging in a line from light strings. Balls A and B are drawn back and released so that they travel towards ball C. Describe and explain the motion. [Assume $e = 1$ and treat the collision between each pair of balls separately.]

[MEI, adapted]

14 A spacecraft has two parts which may separate in flight, the body with mass 15 000 kg and the nose-cone with mass 5000 kg. They rejoin by means of a 'docking' procedure which requires the nose-cone and body to approach along the axis shown in the diagram with a speed of approach of no more than 3 ms^{-1}. If the speed of approach is too great, the linking mechanism will not engage and the two parts will bounce off each other with a speed of separation which is $\frac{1}{4}$ of the speed of approach (i.e. a coefficient of restitution of 0.25). At all times both parts may be taken as travelling in a straight line.

On one occasion the body is travelling forwards at 105 ms^{-1} and the nose-cone forwards at 103 ms^{-1}.

(i) Draw diagrams showing the velocities of the parts before and after docking.
(ii) Calculate the final velocity of the spacecraft.

On another occasion the nose-cone is moving backwards at 5.5 ms^{-1} and the body forwards at 2.5 ms^{-1}.

(iii) Show that the body comes to rest and find the direction and speed of the nose-cone.

After this has happened, before a further attempt to dock is made, the speed of the body is changed in its line of motion by expelling a mass m kg of fuel. The fuel is expelled at a speed of 2000 ms^{-1} and you may assume that all the fuel is expelled instantaneously (i.e. before the body changes speed).

(iv) What value of m would cause the body to have a forward speed of 2.5 ms^{-1} after the fuel is burnt?

[MEI]

Oblique impact with a smooth plane

When an object hits a smooth plane there can be no impulse parallel to the plane so the component of momentum, and hence velocity, is unchanged in this direction. Perpendicular to the plane, the momentum is changed but Newton's law of impact still applies.

The diagrams show the components of the velocity of a ball immediately before and after it hits a smooth plane with coefficient of restitution e.

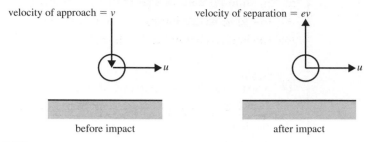

before impact   after impact

Figure 6.22

When the ball is travelling with speed U at an angle α to the plane, the components of the final velocity are $U \cos \alpha$ parallel to the plane and $eU \sin \alpha$, perpendicular to the plane.

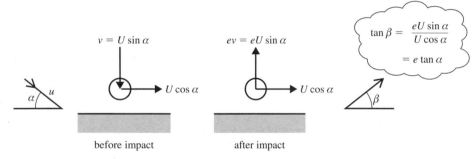

before impact   after impact

Figure 6.23

The *impulse* on the ball is equal to final momentum − initial momentum. This is perpendicular to the plane because there is no change in momentum parallel to the plane.

In figure 6.22 the impulse is

$$mev - m(-v) = (1 + e)\, mv \text{ upwards.}$$

In figure 6.23 the impulse is

$$meU \sin \alpha - m(-U \sin \alpha) = (1 + e)\, mU \sin \alpha \text{ upwards.}$$

Whenever an impact takes place, energy is likely to be lost. In the cases illustrated in the diagrams the *loss in kinetic energy* is

$$\tfrac{1}{2} m \left(u^2 + v^2\right) - \tfrac{1}{2} m \left(u^2 + e^2 v^2\right) = \tfrac{1}{2} m \left(1 - e^2\right) v^2$$

or $\qquad \tfrac{1}{2} m \left(1 - e^2\right) U^2 \sin^2 \alpha$

 What happens to the ball when $e = 0$ and $e = 1$?

EXAMPLE 6.12

A ball of mass $0.2\,\text{kg}$ moving at $12\,\text{ms}^{-1}$ hits a smooth horizontal plane at an angle of $75°$ to the horizontal. The coefficient of restitution is 0.5. Find

(i) the impulse on the ball

(ii) the impulse on the plane

(iii) the kinetic energy lost by the ball.

SOLUTION

(i) The diagram shows the velocities before and after impact.

before impact   after impact

Figure 6.24

Parallel to the plane: $u = 12 \cos 75°$

Perpendicular to the plane: $v = 0.5 \times 12 \sin 75°$ by Newton's law of impact
$= 6 \sin 75°$

The impulse on the ball $=$ final momentum $-$ initial momentum

$$= \begin{pmatrix} 12 \cos 75° \\ 6 \sin 75° \end{pmatrix} - \begin{pmatrix} 12 \cos 75° \\ -12 \sin 75° \end{pmatrix} \text{ (using directions } \mathbf{i}, \mathbf{j} \text{ as shown)}$$

$$= \begin{pmatrix} 0 \\ 18 \sin 75° \end{pmatrix}$$

The impulse on the ball is $18 \sin 75°\,\mathbf{j}$ that is $17.4\,\text{Ns}$ perpendicular to the plane and upwards in the $\mathbf{j}$ direction.

(ii) By Newton's third law, the impulse on the plane is equal and opposite to the impulse on the ball. It is $17.4\,\text{Ns}$ perpendicular to the plane in the direction of $-\mathbf{j}$.

(iii) The initial kinetic energy $= \frac{1}{2} \times 0.2 \times 12^2 = 14.4\,\text{J}$

Final kinetic energy $= \frac{1}{2} \times 0.2 \times [(12 \cos 75°)^2 + (6 \sin 75°)^2]$
$= 4.32\,\text{J}$

Kinetic energy lost $= 14.4 - 4.32 = 10.1\,\text{J}$ (3 sf)

EXERCISE 6D

1 Find the velocity of each of the following after one impact with a smooth plane.

(i) Initial velocity $4\,\text{ms}^{-1}$ at $20°$ to the plane. Coefficient of restitution 0.5.

(ii) Initial velocity $10\,\text{ms}^{-1}$ at $40°$ to the plane. Coefficient of restitution 0.1.

(iii) Initial velocity $u\,\text{ms}^{-1}$ at $\alpha°$ to the plane. Coefficient of restitution 0.8.

2 A ball of mass $0.1\,\text{kg}$ moving at $10\,\text{ms}^{-1}$ hits a smooth horizontal plane at an angle of $80°$ to the horizontal. The coefficient of restitution is 0.6. Find

(i) the impulse on the ball

(ii) the impulse on the plane

(iii) the kinetic energy lost by the ball.

3 A particle of mass 0.05 kg moving at $8\,\text{ms}^{-1}$ hits a smooth horizontal plane at an angle of 45° to the horizontal. The coefficient of restitution is 0. Find
   (i) the impulse on the particle
   (ii) the impulse on the plane
   (iii) the kinetic energy lost by the particle.

4 A ball of mass m kg moving at $u\,\text{ms}^{-1}$ hits a smooth horizontal plane at an angle of $\alpha°$ to the horizontal. The coefficient of restitution is 0.
   (i) Find the impulse on the ball.
   (ii) Show that the kinetic energy lost is $\frac{1}{2}mu^2\sin^2\alpha$.

5 Show that the kinetic energy lost by a particle of mass m kg which hits a smooth plane when it is moving with velocity $u\,\text{ms}^{-1}$ at an angle of $\alpha°$ to the plane is $\frac{1}{2}mu^2(1-e^2)\sin^2\alpha$, where e is the coefficient of restitution.

6 The wind blowing against a sail can be modelled as a series of particles hitting the smooth sail at an angle of 30° and with zero coefficient of restitution. The wind blows at $20\,\text{ms}^{-1}$ and the density of the air is $1.4\,\text{kg m}^{-3}$. Calculate
   (i) the mass of air hitting one square metre of sail each second
   (ii) the impulse of this mass on the sail and hence the force acting on a $2\,\text{m}^2$ sail.

7 A ball is hit from the ground with initial components of velocity $u_1\,\text{ms}^{-1}$ horizontally and $u_2\,\text{ms}^{-1}$ vertically. Assume the ball is a particle and ignore air resistance.
   (i) Show that its horizontal range is $R = \dfrac{2u_1u_2}{g}$

   The ball bounces on the level ground with coefficient of restitution 0.6.
   (ii) How much further does it travel horizontally before the next bounce?
   (iii) Find an expression for the horizontal range after the nth bounce.
   (iv) By considering the sum of a geometric series, calculate the total horizontal distance travelled up to the sixth bounce.

8 A ball is thrown from the origin with a velocity of $10\,\text{ms}^{-1}$ at 60° to the horizontal.
   (i) Calculate its horizontal range, R m.

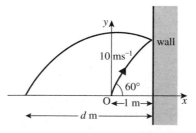

A second ball is thrown from the origin with the same velocity at a smooth vertical wall 1 m away as shown in the diagram. The coefficient of restitution between the ball and the wall is 0.6. Calculate
   (ii) the time taken to reach the wall and the components of a velocity just before and just after the ball hits the wall
   (iii) the value of y when the ball hits the wall

(iv) its distance, d m, from the wall when y is next zero.

(v) Verify that $d = 0.6(R - 1)$.

9 A small marble is projected horizontally over the edge of a table 0.8 m high at a speed of $2.5\,\text{ms}^{-1}$ and bounces on smooth horizontal ground with coefficient of restitution 0.7. Calculate

(i) the components of the velocity of the marble just before it hits the ground

(ii) its horizontal distance from the edge of the table when it first hits the ground

(iii) the horizontal distance travelled between the first and second bounce

(iv) the horizontal distance travelled between the nth and $(n + 1)$th bounces

(v) the number of bounces before the distance between bounces is less than 20 cm.

10 A smooth snooker ball moving at $2\,\text{ms}^{-1}$ hits a cushion at an angle of $30°$ to the cushion. The ball then rebounds and hits a second cushion which is perpendicular to the first. The coefficient of restitution for both impacts is 0.8.

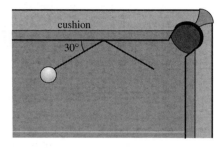

(i) Find the direction of motion after each impact.

(ii) Find the magnitude of the velocity after the second impact.

(iii) Repeat parts (i) and (ii) for a ball moving at $u\,\text{ms}^{-1}$ which hits the first cushion at an angle α. Assume the coefficient of restitution is e. Hence show that the direction of a ball is always reversed after hitting two perpendicular cushions and state the factor by which its speed is reduced.

11 A standard table tennis table is 1.52 m wide and 2.75 m long divided across the middle by a net 15.25 cm high. A ball is served horizontally at $6\,\text{ms}^{-1}$, without spin, from a point 0.3 m above the level of the smooth table. It hits the table at A and then rebounds over the net to hit it again at B. The coefficient of restitution is 0.8.

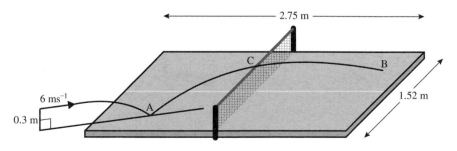

(i) Calculate the length AB.

The ball just passes over the net at a point C.

(ii) Calculate the two possible horizontal distances between B and C.

(iii) Given that B is in fact a point on the shorter edge of the table, find at what angle to the net the ball is served.

1 SUPERBALLS

What happens if a small superball is placed on top of a larger superball, as shown in the diagram, and both balls are dropped together.

Figure 6.25

2 A BOUNCING BALL

Roll a ball off a table and mark the places on the floor where it bounces. Do these give a consistent value for the coefficient of restitution between the ball and the floor?

You may find it helpful to roll the ball down a fixed slope before it leaves the table and to sprinkle talcum powder on the floor so you can see where it lands, or to wet it and have it bounce on a sheet of sugar paper.

3 TABLE TENNIS

How large a room do you need to play table tennis?

KEY POINTS

1 The impulse from a force $\mathbf{F}$ is given by $\mathbf{F}t$ where t is the time for which the force acts. When $\mathbf{F}$ is large and t is small the impulse is denoted by $\mathbf{J}$. Impulse is a vector quantity.

2 The momentum of a body of mass m travelling with velocity $\mathbf{v}$ is given by $m\mathbf{v}$. Momentum is a vector quantity.

3 The impulse–momentum equation is

$$Impulse = final\ momentum - initial\ momentum$$

4 The law of conservation of momentum states that when no external forces are acting on a system, the total momentum of the system is constant. Since momentum is a vector quantity this applies to the magnitude of the momentum in any direction.

5 Coefficient of restitution $e = \dfrac{\text{speed of separation}}{\text{speed of approach}}$

$$speed\ of\ separation = e \times speed\ of\ approach$$

All the above apply perpendicular to a smooth plane.

6 Parallel to a smooth plane the velocity is unchanged.

7 The S.I. unit for impulse and momentum is the newton second (Ns).

7 Frameworks

I have yet to see any problem, however complicated, which, when looked at in the right way, did not become still more complicated.

Paul Anderson

The Millennium Stadium at Cardiff has been built using frameworks made from triangular elements. You will have seen many structures like this.

 Why is the triangle the basic element in so many structures?

This chapter is concerned with the forces in structural frameworks. Not all structures are based on frameworks, but many are because the strength to weight ratio for a framework is usually higher than for a solid structure.

A framework is an arrangement of structural members (rods or cables). Frameworks are almost always made from triangular elements fitted together in two or three dimensions, because a triangle is rigid even if it is freely hinged (or *pin-jointed*) at the corners. If any other shape, such as a quadrilateral, were used, the joints would have to be rigid. This would make both the design of the structure and its successful construction far more difficult.

To analyse the forces in frameworks is quite complex, unless you can make two simplifying assumptions.

(i) All members of the framework are light, so that their masses can be ignored;

(ii) All the joints are smooth pin joints. This means that the bars could rotate about the joints without any resistance: there are no moments acting at the joints.

The consequence of these assumptions is that all the internal forces are directed along the rods. Then the only forces that need to be considered are the external forces on the framework, and the tensions or thrusts in the rods of the framework.

? ABCDE is a framework of seven light freely jointed rods, all of the same length, supported at A and D. A weight of 1000 N is hanging from E.

Which of the rods do you think are in tension and which in compression (thrust)?

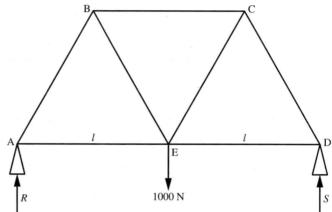

Figure 7.1

Now follow the analysis of this structure in the worked example below and see whether your intuitive ideas were correct.

EXAMPLE 7.1 Calculate the forces in each of the rods in the structure above, stating whether the rod is in tension or compression.

SOLUTION

(i) External forces
There are three external forces acting on the framework, RN and SN vertically upwards and 1000 N vertically downwards. Looking at the equilibrium of the structure as a whole:

For vertical equilibrium:	$R + S = 1000$	①
Taking moments about A:	$R \times 2l = 1000 \times l$	
$\Rightarrow$	$R = 500$	
From ①	$S = 500$	

Notice that you could have found this result by symmetry of framework and forces.

(ii) Internal forces

The next step is to mark the internal forces acting on the joints. In this case they are all unknown and all the rods are assumed to be in tension, as in figure 7.2. If in fact the forces are thrusts they will be found to have negative values.

The tensions (in N) have been called T_1, T_2, T_3, ..., T_7. They could equally have been called T_{AB}, T_{AE}, ..., T_{CD}.

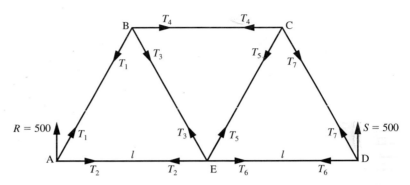

Figure 7.2

Now consider the equilibrium of each joint in turn. It is best to avoid joints where there are more than two unknowns, so start at A or D.

Starting with A (figure 7.3):

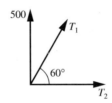

Figure 7.3

Vertical equilibrium: $T_1 \sin 60° + 500 = 0$
$$\Rightarrow \quad T_1 = -577 \text{ (thrust).} \quad ①$$
Horizontal equilibrium: $T_1 \cos 60° + T_2 = 0$
$$-577 \cos 60° + T_2 = 0$$
$$\Rightarrow \quad T_2 = 289 \text{ (tension).} \quad ②$$

Moving on to point B (figure 7.4):

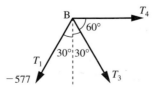

Figure 7.4

Vertical equilibrium: $T_1 \cos 30° + T_3 \cos 30° = 0$
Substitute from ① $-577 \cos 30° + T_3 \cos 30° = 0$
$$\Rightarrow \qquad\qquad\qquad T_3 = 577 \text{ (tension).} \quad ③$$

Horizontal equilibrium: $\quad T_4 + T_3 \cos 60° - T_1 \cos 60° = 0$

$\Rightarrow \qquad\qquad\qquad\qquad T_4 + 577 \cos 60° + 577 \cos 60° = 0$

$\Rightarrow \qquad\qquad\qquad\qquad\qquad\qquad\qquad T_4 = -577 \text{ (thrust).} \quad \text{④}$

The three remaining tensions can be deduced because both the framework and the external forces are symmetrical about the vertical through E.

$T_7 = T_1 = -577$ (thrust); $T_5 = T_3 = 577$ (tension): $T_6 = T_2 = 289$ (tension).

Alternatively you can find them by considering the equilibrium of the other joints.

Figure 7.5 shows the forces in all of the members.

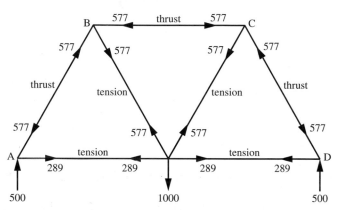

Figure 7.5

EXAMPLE 7.2

Figure 7.6 shows a simple crane. AB is a cable; BC, CD and DB are light freely jointed rods. The framework is freely hinged to its base at D. A load of 5000 N is hanging from C. The rod CD and the cable BA both make angles of 45° with the horizontal and BC is horizontal. Find exact values for

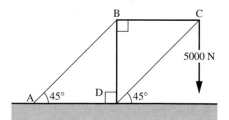

Figure 7.6

(i)   the tension in the cable AB
(ii) the magnitude of the reaction of the base on the framework at D
(iii) the force in each rod, stating whether it is in tension or compression.

SOLUTION

(i)   The diagram shows the external forces.

Assume that BD and BC are of length a units.

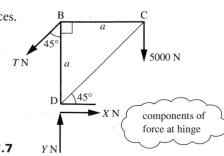

Figure 7.7

Taking moments about D for the whole framework:

$$T \sin 45° \times a = 5000 \times a$$

$$\Rightarrow \qquad T = 5000\sqrt{2} \qquad \boxed{\sin 45° = \frac{1}{\sqrt{2}}}$$

The tension in the cable AB is $5000\sqrt{2}$ N.

(ii) Resolving horizontally:

$$X = T \sin 45°$$

$$\Rightarrow \qquad X = 5000$$

Resolving vertically:

$$Y = T \cos 45° + 5000$$

$$\Rightarrow \qquad Y = 10\,000. \qquad \boxed{\cos 45° = \frac{1}{\sqrt{2}}}$$

The magnitude of the reaction at D is $5000\sqrt{(1^2 + 2^2)} = 5000\sqrt{5}$ N.

(iii) The diagram shows all the internal and external forces on the joints.

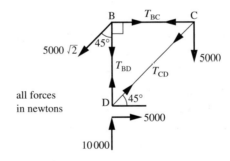

Figure 7.8

For B, vertically: $\qquad T_{BD} + 5000\sqrt{2} \times \cos 45° = 0$

$$T_{BD} = -5000$$

horizontally: $\qquad T_{BC} - 5000\sqrt{2} \times \sin 45° = 0$

$$T_{BC} = 5000.$$

For C, vertically: $\qquad T_{CD} \cos 45° - 5000 = 0$

$$T_{CD} = 5000\sqrt{2}.$$

The stresses in the rods are BD: 5000 N (compression), BC: 5000 N (tension), CD: $5000\sqrt{2}$ N (compression).

These values are exact. The compression in CD can now be written to any required degree of accuracy.

The illustration shows a framework formed from an experimental structures kit.

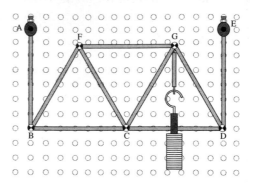

Figure 7.9

(i) For the structure, predict which rods are in tension and which rods are in compression.

(ii) Which rods could be replaced by strings?

(iii) You will see that there is a load applied to the structure. Calculate the force in each rod when the mass of the load is 200 g.

(iv) Make the structure from a kit, or other suitable equipment. Replace each rod in turn with a force meter to check your predictions.

1 The diagram shows a framework made up of three light rods which are freely jointed at A, B and C. A load of 2000 N is applied at the point B.

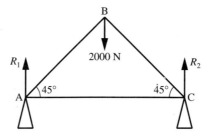

(i) Find the magnitudes of the forces R_1 and R_2.

(ii) Draw a sketch of the framework and mark in tensions T_1, T_2 and T_3 acting in the rods AB, BC and CA respectively.

(iii) If one of these rods is actually in compression, how will the value of the tension show this?

(iv) Write down equations for the horizontal and vertical equilibrium of joint A and solve these equations to find T_1 and T_3.

(v) By considering the equilibrium of joint B, find T_2.

(vi) Show that with the values of T_2 and T_3 which you have found, joint C is also in equilibrium.

(vii) Write down the forces in the three rods, stating whether they are in tension or in compression.

2 A framework LMN consists of three light, freely jointed rods LM, MN and NL. Their lengths (in m) are as shown in the diagram. The framework is suspended from the points L and M by vertical strings with tensions S_1 and S_2 N and a weight of 1500 N is hung from N. The rod LM is horizontal.

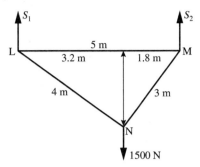

(i) Find the tensions S_1 and S_2.

(ii) Draw a sketch of the framework and mark in tensions T_1, T_2 and T_3 acting in the rods LM, MN and NL respectively.

(iii) Write down equations for the horizontal and vertical equilibrium of point M and solve these equations to find T_1 and T_2.

(iv) By considering the equilibrium of point N, find T_3.

(v) Show that with the values of T_1 and T_3 which you have found, point L is also in equilibrium.

(vi) Write down the forces in the three rods, stating whether they are in tension or in compression.

3 Two 100 N weights are suspended from the points B and C of the light pin-jointed framework ABC shown. The angles ABC and ACB are both 30°. The framework is itself suspended by a light string attached to A.

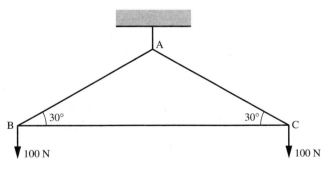

(i) Write down the three external forces acting on the framework.

(ii) Find the internal forces in the three rods, AB, AC and BC and state whether they are in tension or compression.

4 The diagram shows a framework PQR of light, freely jointed rods in the shape of an equilateral triangle. The framework is freely hinged to the wall at P. A light string connecting Q to S is taut when QS and PR are horizontal, as in the diagram. A weight of 500 N is hanging from R.

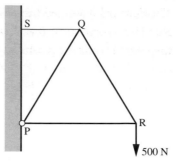

(i) By considering the equilibrium of the whole framework PQR, find the tension in the string QS.

(ii) Find the reaction of the wall on the framework at P
  (a) as horizontal and vertical components
  (b) in magnitude and direction form.

(iii) Find the internal forces in the three rods, stating whether they are in tension or in compression.

5 The diagram shows a crane supporting a load of 2000 N. The framework is light and freely jointed, and is secured at points A and C.
  (i) Find the external forces acting on the framework.
  (ii) Find the force in each member of the framework stating whether it is in tension or compression.

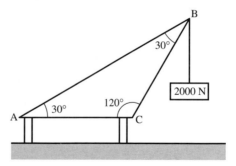

6 The diagram shows a framework of light, freely jointed rods supported at its base and carrying a load of 2500 N at its top. Find the force in each of the five rods, stating whether it is in tension or in compression.

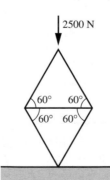

(i) Make two- and three-dimensional structures from a kit and investigate the forces acting in your structures.

(ii) **The Forth Railway Bridge**

The photograph shows a living model of the Forth Bridge at the time of its construction: 'the chairs a third of a mile apart, the mens' heads 360 ft above ground'. Investigate this structure.

KEY POINTS

Method for solving framework problems

1 First calculate the external forces acting on a framework.
   • Consider the horizontal and vertical equilibrium of the whole framework.
   • Take moments about a suitable point for the whole framework.

2 Then calculate the internal forces making these two *assumptions*:
   • all the members of the framework are light rods;
   • all the joints are smooth so there are no moments acting on them.

3 Consider the horizontal and vertical equilibrium of each joint in turn. Make sure that there are no more than two unknown forces each time you move to a new joint.

Answers

Chapter 1

❓ (Page 1)

Assumptions: motorcycle is a particle, uniform frictional force with road, horizontal, linear motion with constant deceleration.
See also text which follows

❓ (Page 4)

Downward slope would extend skid so u is an overestimate; opposite for upward slope. Air resistance would reduce skid so u is an underestimate. Smaller μ would extend skid so u is an overestimate.

❓ (Page 4)

Friction is forwards when pedalling, backwards when freewheeling.

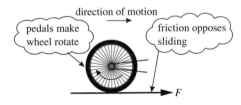

Exercise 1A (Page 8)

1 (i) 0.1   (ii) 0.5
2 (i) $F = 2g$
   (ii) $2.45\,\mathrm{ms}^{-2}$
   (iii) $F = 2g$
   (iv) $2.205\,\mathrm{ms}^{-2}$
3 4.80 kN
4 (i) $1.02\,\mathrm{ms}^{-2}$
   (ii) 0.102 N
   (iii) 0.104
   (iv) 49 m; independent of mass
5 0.816

6 (i) smoother contact
   (ii) 0.2
   (iii) 137 N
7 (i) $7.35\,\mathrm{ms}^{-2}$
   (ii) $17.7\,\mathrm{ms}^{-2}$
   (iii) 59.9 m
8 (i) 58.8 N
   (ii) 62.5 N
9 (i) 0.577
   (ii) 35°
   (iii) 2.14
   (iv) 50.2°
10 (i)

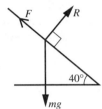

   (ii) $4.42\,\mathrm{ms}^{-2}$
   (iii) $5.15\,\mathrm{ms}^{-1}$
   (iv) 5.42 m
11 (i)

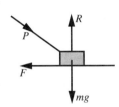

   (ii) 73.3° F/R does not change
   (iii) 25.0 N
   (iv) No, the wheels do not slip.
12 greater than, equal to, less than 16.7°, respectively
13 (i) 5.68 N
   (ii) Block accelerates down slope until $T = 0.196$ then slows down.
14 (i) 0.194
   (ii) $4.84\,\mathrm{ms}^{-2}$
   (iii) $9.84\,\mathrm{ms}^{-1}$
   (iv) $9.85\,\mathrm{ms}^{-1}$
15 (i)

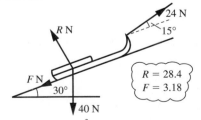

   (iii) 3.46 N, $4.05\,\mathrm{ms}^{-2}$

16 (i) (a) 37.9 N **(b)** 37.2 N **(c)** 37.5 N

(ii) $\dfrac{40}{\cos\alpha + 0.4\sin\alpha}$

(iii) 21.8°

Chapter 2

❷ (Page 15)

If you can add more, the block is likely to accelerate when displaced. In this case the coefficient of friction is slightly larger in the limiting (static) case than when the block is sliding.

❷ (Page 16)

Constant acceleration requires that the friction is uniform over the surface of the plane, the pulley is smooth and light, the string is light and inextensible and that there is no air resistance. Also, Coulomb's law of friction is assumed.

❷ (Page 17)

See text which follows.

❷ (Page 18)

Consistently slow reaction times or consistently pressing the button too soon. Reaction times create the largest errors in this experiment.

❷ (Page 18)

Lack of concentration. You cannot ignore an outlier which is a genuine measurement.

❷ (Page 19)

These could indicate that P's early measurements were in fact too small.

❷ (Page 20)

It does not use all the data; large variations in measuring smaller times are ignored.

❷ (Page 21)

Squaring t makes the errors larger; m_1, $m_1 + m_2$ and s.

Exercise 2A (Page 23)

1 (i) $2.35 \leqslant d < 2.45$

(ii) $4095 \leqslant M < 4105$

(iii) $53 \leqslant t < 55$

2 (i) $8.55 \leqslant x + y < 9.65$

(ii) $0.425 \leqslant xy < 1.425$

(iii) $8.35 < x - y < 9.45$

(iv) $56.66 < \frac{x}{y} < 190$

3 (i) 27.5 km

(ii) $25.375 \leqslant s < 29.71$

(iii) You can be sure of 1 sf

(iv) 28 km

4 (i) 55.2 km h^{-1}

(ii) $114.5 \leqslant s < 115.5$, $124.5 \leqslant t < 125.5$

(iii) $54.74 < \text{av. speed} < 55.66$

(iv) 2 sf

5 (i) 30.6 m

(ii) $29.38 < s < 31.89$

(iii) 31 m

(iv) Air resistance would slow down the stone.

6 (i) 8.6 ms^{-2}

    (a) The method is not accurate because air resistance is ignored.

    (b) It is not reliable because wind and up-currents vary.

(ii) $7.09, 10.64 \text{ ms}^{-2}$; Timing inaccuracy might affect results more

7 (i) (a) 9.780 **(b)** 9.812 **(c)** 9.809

(ii) 308 m

8 (ii) $u = 27$, $d = 19.035$; $u = 33$, $d = 26.235$; $u = 30$, $d = 22.5$; 15.4%, 16.6%.

(iii) $u = 63$, $d = 78.435$; $u = 77$, $d = 112.035$; $u = 70$, $d = 94.5$; 17%, 18.6%. $u = 90$, $d = 148.5$; $u = 110$, $d = 214.5$; $u = 100$, $d = 180$; 17.5%, 19.2%.

(iv) Errors increase with u, 10% is too great. Perhaps 5 mph at all speeds would be better.

9 (i) and (ii)

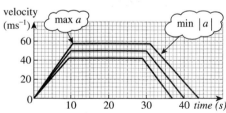

(iii) 1500 m, 1203 m, 1858 m

(iv) 19.8%, 23.9%; a, 10%, t_1, 5%, t_2, 2.5%

Chapter 3

❷ (Page 29)

(i) The tool shown in figure 3.9(i) works with one hand but has less leverage (moment). See also text.

❓ (Page 35)

(i) $P + Q$ line of action parallel to P and Q and in same direction; distance from O is

$$a + \frac{bQ}{P + Q} \text{ (between } P \text{ and } Q)$$

(ii) $P - Q$ line of action parallel to P and Q and in direction of the larger; distance from O is

$$a - \frac{bQ}{P - Q} \text{ (to the left of } P \text{ for } P > Q)$$

❓ (Page 35)

You produce equal and opposite couples using friction between one hand and the lid and between the other hand and the jar so that they turn in opposite directions. Pressing increases the normal reactions and hence the maximum friction possible.

Exercise 3A (Page 35)

1 (a) 15 Nm   **(b)** −22 Nm   **(c)** 18 Nm   **(d)** −28 Nm

2 (a) 2.1 Nm   **(b)** 6.16 Nm   **(c)** 0.1 Nm   **(d)** 0.73 Nm

3 28.6 N, 20.4 N

4 96.5 N, 138.5 N

5 (i) 1225 N, 1225 N
  (ii) 1449 N, 1785 N

6 (i) 55 kg

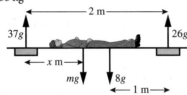

  (ii) 0.8 m

7 (i) $P = 27.5g$, $Q = 147.5g$
  (ii) $P = 2.5g$, $Q = 172.5g$
  (iii) If child is less than 0.95 m from the adult, $P < 0$ so the bench tips unless A is anchored to the ground.
  (iv) The bench tips if A is not anchored.

8 (i) $15g$ N, $30g$ N
  (ii) $90g$ N, $5g$ N
  (iii) zero
  (iv) $\frac{2}{3}$ m

9 (i) $0.5g(30 - x)$ kN, $0.5g(20 + x)$ kN
  (ii) its centre of mass
  (iii) constant $15g$ kN each.

10 (i) $35g$ N, $75g$ N
  (ii) no
  (iii) 36 kg

11 (i) 2262 N, 7538 N
  (ii) 6
  (iii) 784 N

12 (i) 4800 N
  (ii) 0.0023 ms^{-2}
  (iii) 947 N

❓ (Page 43)

No, the system is symmetrical providing the rod is uniform.

❓ (Page 47)

The simplest is: resolve ↑ for BC to find R then take moments about B for T.

Exercise 3B (Page 47)

1 (i) 6 Nm
  (ii) −10.7 Nm
  (iii) 23 Nm
  (iv) 0
  (v) −4.24 Nm
  (vi) 4.24 Nm

2 David and Hannah (by radius × 0.027 Nm)

3 (i) 5915 kg
  (ii) $4532 \sec \theta$ kg

4 (i) 42.4 N
  (ii) 27.7 N
  (iii) 30.1 N

5 (i) $T \cos 30°$, $T \sin 30°$
  (iii) 30 Nm
  (v) 8.04 N, 15.36 N
  (vi) (a) 33.7°   **(b)** 3.23 m

6 (i) 1405 N
  (ii) 638 N, 1612 N
  (iv) (a) jib stays put, $T = 0$ **(b)** A drops

7 (i)

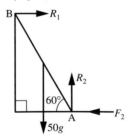

  (ii) 0
  (iii) 141 N
  (iv) 141 N, $\mu \leqslant 0.289$

8 (i)

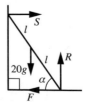

  (a) (ii) 56.6, 56.6, 196   **(iii)** 0.29
  (b) (ii) 98, 98, 196   **(iii)** 0.5

9 (i)

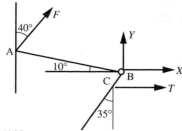

(ii) 162 N

(iii) 61.7 N

10 (ii) 1 600 000 Nm

(iii) 6830 N, 3830 N

11 (i) See Example 3.6 page 45

(ii)

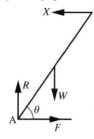

(v) AC should be small for a slippery surface.

12 (i)

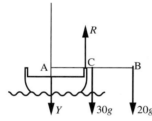

(ii) $80g = 784$ N

(iii) $30g = 294$ N vertically down

(iv) $17.5g$ N

13 (i)

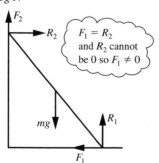

$F_1 = R_2$
and R_2 cannot
be 0 so $F_1 \neq 0$

(ii) (b) $32g$ N

14 (i)

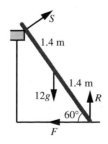

(ii) 25.5 N, 103 N

(iii) 0.51

(iv) 2.25 m

15 (i)

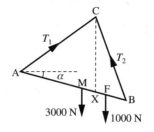

(ii) 0.25 m, 0.75 m; 4 m, 3.6°

(iii) 2290 N, 2700 N

(iv) 10.6°

16 (i) 19.4°

(ii) $\tan \phi = 2 \tan \theta$

❓ (Page 53)

It is likely to topple. Toppling depends on relative mass of upstairs and downstairs passengers.

❓ (Page 54)

1st slide, 2nd topple.

❓ (Page 54)

R cannot act outside the surfaces in contact so there is a resultant moment about the edge E.

❓ (Page 56)

Yes, when $\mu = 0.5$ and $\alpha = 26.6$

Exercise 3C (Page 57)

1 (i) $2.8g$ N

(ii) $3.5g$ N

(iii) slide

2 (i) $P = 2\mu g$

(ii) $0.6g$ N

(iii) $\mu < 0.3$

(iv) $\mu > 0.3$

3 It slides.

4 (a) (i) 22.5 N

(ii) 22.0 N

(iii) topples

(b) (i) 22.8 N

(ii) 25.9 N

(iii) slides. 63.4°, 22.4 N

5 (i) 14.0°

(ii) 18.4°

(iii) sliding

6 (i) (a) 50 by 20   **(b)** 20 by 10
  (ii) not at all if faces identical
  (iii) (a) $\mu < 0.2$ **(b)** $\mu > 5$
7 (i) stays put
  (ii) topples
8 (ii) $P\sin\theta$, $\mu(150 - P\cos\theta)$
  (iii) acts through a point on AB
  (v) $\mu < \tan\theta$

Chapter 4

❓ (Page 61)

Yes, centre of mass vertically below P.

❓ (Page 61)

Vertically above bar.

❓ (Page 63)

$4 \times 1\frac{2}{15} + 5 \times \frac{2}{15} = 6 \times \frac{13}{15}$

Exercise 4A (Page 66)
1 (i) 0.2 m
  (ii) 0
  (iii) −0.72 m
  (iv) 1.19 m
  (v) +0.275 M
  (vi) 0.36 m
  (vii) −0.92 m
  (viii) 0.47 m
2 2.18 m from 20 kg child
3 4.2 cm
4 4680 km
5 0.92 m
6 3.33 mm from centre
7 2.95 cm
8 1.99 kg
9 42 kg
10 $\dfrac{m_2 l}{(m_1 + m_2)}$ from m_1 end
11 (i) 3.35 m, tips over
  (ii) 4.55 tonnes
  (iii) $L(l - d) < Md + C(a + d)$, $C(a - d) < Md$
  (iv) $\dfrac{2Mad}{(l - d)(a - d)}$

Exercise 4B (Page 73)
1 (i) (2.3, −0.3)
  (ii) (0, 1.75)
  (iii) $(\frac{1}{24}, \frac{1}{6})$
  (iv) (−2.7, −1.5)

2 $(5, 6\frac{1}{3})$
3 (i) (20, 60)
  (ii) (30, 65)
  (iii) (30, 60)
4 23 cm
5 (i) (a) (1.5, −1.5)   **(b)** (1.5, −2.05)
  (ii) $(1\frac{5}{12}, -1\frac{1}{2}, \frac{1}{12})$
6 (i) (28, 60)
  (ii) (52, 60)
  (iii) (64, 60)
  (iv) 40 cm
7 (i) 0.5 m from ground
  (ii) 16.7°
  (iv) 19.4 kg
8 (i) (a) (10, 2.5)   **(b)** (12.5, 5)   **(c)** (15, 7.5)
    (d) (17.5, 10)   **(e)** (20, 12.5)
  (ii) 5
  (iii) $(9 + n, 2.5n)$, 11
  (iv) 102.5 cm
9 (i) 0.2 cm below O
  (ii) 9.1°
10 (i) $(0.5a, 1.2a)$
  (ii) 3.9°
  (iii) $2m$
11 (i) 2.25
  (ii) 0.56 m
  (iii) 0.40, $(\frac{1}{2}, 1\frac{1}{2})$
12 (i) (4.06, 2)
  (ii) (3.31, 2, 0.74)
  (iii) topples, line from G to ABIJ is $> 90°$ to hor.
13 (i) $(3\frac{1}{4}, 2\frac{1}{6})$
  (ii) $(3\frac{1}{6}, 2\frac{1}{6})$
  (iii) $(2\frac{7}{12}, 2\frac{1}{6}, \frac{1}{2})$
14 (i) curved face when $\theta < 113°$
  (iii) stays put
  (iv) rolls over (G right of E)
15 (i) (a) $\dfrac{(4m + M)h}{8m + 4M}$ **(b)** $\dfrac{h(M\alpha^2 + m)}{2(M\alpha + m)}$

Chapter 5

❓ (Page 82)

The machine never stops (never loses energy).
No, it is an optical illusion.

Exercise 5A (Page 89)
1 (i) 2500 J
  (ii) 40 000 J
  (iii) 5.6×10^9 J
  (iv) 3.7×10^{28} J
  (v) 10^{-25} J

2 (i)   1000 J
  (ii) 1070 J
  (iii) 930 J
  (iv) None
3 (i)   4320 J
  (ii) 4320 J
  (iii) 144 N
4 (i)   540 000 J, No
  (ii) 3600 N
5 (i)   500 000 J
  (ii) 6667 N
6 (i)   (a) 5250 J   (b) −13 750 J
  (ii) (a) 495 250 J   (b) 476 250 J
7 (i)   64 J
  (ii) dissipated
  (iii) 64 J
  (iv) 400 N
  (v)   89.4 ms^{-1}
8 (i) 3.146×10^5 J
  (ii) 8.28×10^3 N
  (iii) dissipated as heat and sound
  (iv) some of work is dissipated.
9 18.6 ms^{-1}
10 (i) 240 N
  (ii) 5.5 m
  (iii) 1320 J
  (iv) 270 J
  (v)   960 J, 90 J

❓ (Page 96)

More work cycling into the wind, less if at an angle, minimum if wind behind.

Exercise 5B (Page 98)

1 (i)   9.8 J
  (ii) 94.5 J
  (iii) −58.8 J
  (iv) −58.9 J
2 (i)   −27.44 J
  (ii) 54.9 J
  (iii) −11.8 J
3 17.6 J
4 23 300 J
5 (i)   154 000 J
  (ii) 20 000 J
  (iii) distance moved against gravity is $200 \sin 5°$
  (iv) 138 000 J
6 (i)   (a) 1500 J   (b) 280 J
  (ii) (a) 15.6 ms^{-1} (b) 16.1 ms^{-1}
7 (i)   2120 J
  (ii) the same

8 (i)   (a) 1700 J   (b) 8.7 ms^{-1}
  (ii) (a) unaltered   (b) decreased
9 (i)   1750 J
  (ii) 1750 J, 8.37 ms^{-1}
  (iii) 50°
  (iv) it is always perpendicular to the motion
10 (i) 154 J
  (ii) $153.7 - 1.96x$
  (iii) $0 \leqslant t \leqslant 4$
  (iv) 27.7 ms^{-1}
  (v)   58.8 m
11 (i) 34 300 J, 21 875 J
  (ii) 248.5 N
  (iii) 5061 N
12 (i) 9.8 ms^{-2}
  (ii) $1.47(10t - 4.9t^2), 0 \leqslant t \leqslant 2.04$
  (iii) 5.1 m, 10$\mathbf{i}$
  (iv) $10\mathbf{i} + 10\mathbf{j}$, 14.1 ms^{-1}, 15 J
  (v)   No air resistance; No
13 (i) 109 ms^{-1}
  (ii) 115 N
  (iii) The heavier (relatively less affected by resistance).
14 (i) 12 J, 8.76 J
  (ii) 3.24 J
  (iii) 0.217 N
  (iv) 14.1 ms^{-1}
15 (i) 20 ms^{-1}
  (iii) 250 m
  (iv) $20M$ kN
16 (i) 592 J
  (ii) 759 000 J
  (iii) 211 W
17 (i) 5 m
  (ii) 6.26 ms^{-1}
  (iii) 8 m
  (iv) Yvette is a particle and remains upright. No air resistance.

Exercise 5C (Page 105)

1 (i)   308.7 J
  (ii) 37 044 J
  (iii) 10.3 W
2 (i)   2352 J
  (ii) 1176 W
  (iii) 1882 W, 0 W, 2822 W
3 (i)   31 752 J
  (ii) 16 200 J
  (iii) 1598 J
  (iv) 1332 N
  (v)   power = 1598 J
4 (i)   703 N
  (ii) mass of car

5 576 N

6 245 kW

7 (i)   560 W

(ii) 168 000 J

8 (i)   1250 J

(ii) 209 W

9 (i)   20 ms^{-1}

(ii) 0.0125 ms^{-1}

(iii) 25 ms^{-1}

10 (i) 1.6×10^7 W

(ii) 0.0025 ms^{-2}

(iii) 5.7 ms^{-1}

11 (i)   16

(ii) 320 N

(iii) 6400 W

(iv) (a) 1.98 ms^{-2} (b) 0.97 ms^{-2}

12 (i)   9800 N, 9750 N

(ii) 3020 N

(iii) 50.4 kW

(iv) 95.2 km h^{-1}

13 (i)   61 300 J

(ii) 511 W

(iii) 46.9 s

Chapter 6

? (Page 110)

Use $v = u + at$ to find average acceleration then $\mathbf{F} = m\mathbf{a}$.
Average force = assumed constant force
Answer in text.

? (Page 111)

Ball: mom. 6 Ns, K.E. 120 J;
truck: mom. 200 Ns, K.E. 1 J.
Low momentum better.

Exercise 6A (Page 117)

1 (i)   500 Ns

(ii) 20 000 Ns

(iii) 2.8×10^8 Ns

(iv) 2×10^{-22} Ns

2 (i)   18 200 Ns

(ii) 0.002 25 Ns

(iii) 3 Ns

(iv) 10 Ns

3 (i)   15 N

(ii) 20 m

(iii) 20 ms^{-1}

(iv) 300 J. Work = K.E. gain

(v) 30 Ns, impulse = mom. gain

4 (i)   1.2 Ns upwards

(ii) 2 s

(iii) 0

(iv) 1.2 Ns

5 (i)   2.125 Ns

(ii) (a) 21.25 N   (b) 42.5 N

(iii) smaller impulse on hands

6 (i)   11 900 Ns

(ii) 99 000 N

(iii) 11g

(iv) lower deceleration

7 (i)   5.42 ms^{-1}

(ii) 108.4 Ns

(iii) 108.4 Ns

(iv) 542 N

8 (i)   +30 000 Ns

(ii) −15 000 Ns

(iii) −45 000 Ns

(iv) the impulse

(v) 450 000 N

9 (i)

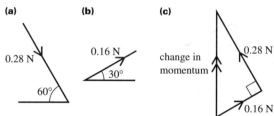

(iii) $1.75\mathbf{i} - 3.03\mathbf{j}$, $1.73\mathbf{i} + \mathbf{j}$

(iv) 0.32 Ns at 90.3°. There is hardly any change in momentum parallel to the cushion.

10 (i)   −20$\mathbf{i}$

(ii) $5.1\mathbf{i} + 0.6\mathbf{j} + 0.45\mathbf{k}$

(iii) Fatima

11 (i)   (a) 0.048 Ns right   (b) 0.048 Ns left

(ii) 0.432 N

12 (i)   the impulse of the force

(ii) 12 250 Ns

(iii) 4.9 ms^{-1}

? (Page 120)

Answer in text.

? (Page 122)

Van $\frac{1}{4}$ m, car $-\frac{3}{8}$ m. Crumpling better to absorb energy.

Exercise 6B (Page 126)

1 195 ms^{-1}

2 (i)   2 ms^{-1}

(ii) 1.5 ms^{-1}

3 **(i)** $25.6\,\text{ms}^{-1}$

   (ii) 4440 Ns forwards

   (iii) 4440 Ns backwards

4 **(i)** $1\frac{2}{3}\,\text{ms}^{-1}$

   (ii) 1670 Ns forwards on car, backwards on lorry

5 **(i)** $0.623\,\text{ms}^{-1}$

   (ii) 9.97 Ns

   (iii) 997 N

6 **(i)** $4990\,\text{ms}^{-1}$

   (ii) $5000.001\,\text{ms}^{-1}$

7 **(i)** $3\,\text{ms}^{-1}$

   (ii) Impulse 1500 Ns is too great

8 **(i)** 0

   (ii) M: $-0.75\,\text{ms}^{-1}$, A: $1.05\,\text{ms}^{-1}$

   (iii) M: $-52.5\,$Ns, A: $+52.5\,$Ns

   (iv) 0

9 **(i)** $1\,\text{ms}^{-1}$

   (ii) $9\,\text{ms}^{-1}$

   (iii) $21\,\text{ms}^{-1}$

   (iv) $33\,\text{ms}^{-1}$

10 **(i)** 49 000 J

   (ii) $7\,\text{ms}^{-1}$

   (iii) $4\,\text{ms}^{-1}$

   (iv) 42.9%.

11 **(i)** $10\,\text{ms}^{-1}$

   (ii) 24 000 Ns

   (iii) 24 000 Ns

   (iv) 966 000 N

   (v) 0.5 m

12 **(i)** $9495\,\text{ms}^{-1}$

   (ii) 4.51×10^7 J

   (iii) 3.76×10^8 N

13 **(i)** $0.196\,\text{ms}^{-1}$

   (ii) $0.385\,\text{ms}^{-1}$

   (iv)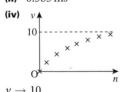

    $v \to 10$

   (v) faster, ball has negative momentum.

14 **(i)** $\frac{2}{3}\,\text{ms}^{-1}$

   (iii) true

? **(Page 129)**

No, cricket ball bounces lower. Second bounces lower.

Exercise 6C (Page 133)

1 **(i)** $\frac{2}{3}$

   (ii) $1.44\,\text{ms}^{-1}$

   (iii) $\frac{3}{4}$

   (iv) $3.2\,\text{ms}^{-1}$

2 **(i)** 0.3

   (ii) 0

   (iii) 0.95

   (iv) 1

3 **(i)** 0.8

   (ii) 1.62 Ns

   (iii) 2.43 J

4 **(i)** $4.43\,\text{ms}^{-1}$

   (ii) $3.98\,\text{ms}^{-1}$

   (iii) 0.9

   (iv) 0.149 J

   (v) 0.149 J

   (vi) 0.656 m

5 **(i)** $1\,\text{ms}^{-1}$

   (ii) 0.2

   (iii) 450 Ns

   (iv) 900 J

6 **(i)** $20\,\text{ms}^{-1}$

   (ii) $\frac{3}{4}$

   (iii) 1750 Ns

   (iv) 4375 J

   (v) low

7 **(a)** **(ii)** $2.5\,\text{ms}^{-1}$, $3.5\,\text{ms}^{-1}$ **(iii)** 3.75 J

   (b) **(ii)** -0.5, $2.5\,\text{ms}^{-1}$ **(iii)** 33.75 J

   (c) **(ii)** $1.2\,\text{ms}^{-1}$, $1.2\,\text{ms}^{-1}$ **(iv)** 4.8 J

   (d) **(ii)** $-1\,\text{ms}^{-1}$, $2\,\text{ms}^{-1}$ **(iv)** 0 J

   (e) **(ii)** $-0.5\,\text{ms}^{-1}$, $1\,\text{ms}^{-1}$ **(iv)** 2.25 J

   (f) **(ii)** $2\,\text{ms}^{-1}$, $4\,\text{ms}^{-1}$ **(iv)** 96 J

8 **(i)**

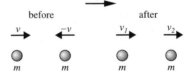

   (ii) $-ev$, ev

9 $\frac{13}{32}$, $\frac{15}{32}$, $\frac{9}{8}$

10 $-\frac{47}{16}$, $\frac{7}{16}$

11 **(ii)** $2\,\text{ms}^{-1}$

   (iii) $\frac{2}{3}$

   (v) $m_1 \leqslant m_2$

   (vi) $e : 1$, 1

12 **(i)** $\sqrt{\frac{2h}{g}}$, $\sqrt{2gh}$

   (ii) $e^2 h$

   (iii) $h e^{2n}$

   (iv) $\sqrt{\left(\frac{2h}{g}\right)(1+2e)}$,

    $\left(\sqrt{\frac{2h}{g}}\right)(1+2e+\ldots+2e^{n-1})$

   (vi) $\dfrac{h(1+e^2)}{(1-e^2)}$

13 **(ii)** A, B at rest, C at speed u

   (iii) E speed u remainder at rest

   (iv) D, E move together with initial speed of A, B, others at rest.

14 (i)

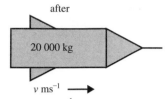

before

after

(ii) 104.5 ms^{-1}
(iii) 2 ms^{-1} forwards
(iv) 18.75 kg

? (Page 138)

When $e = 0$ the ball slides with speed u against the surface, though a small amount of friction might make it roll. When $e = 1$, no energy is lost and the angles α and β are equal as for a ray of light.

Exercise 6D (Page 139)

1 (i) 3.82 ms^{-1} at 10.3° to the plane
 (ii) 7.69 ms^{-1} at 4.8° to the plane
 (iii) $u\sqrt{\cos^2\alpha + 0.64\sin^2\alpha}$
  $= u\sqrt{1 - 0.36\sin^2\alpha}$ ms^{-1} at β° to the plane;
  $\tan\beta = 0.8\tan\alpha$
2 (i) 1.58 Ns vertically upwards
 (ii) 1.58 Ns vertically downwards
 (iii) 3.1 J
3 (i) 0.283 N vertically upwards
 (ii) 0.283 N vertically downwards
 (iii) 0.8 J
4 (i) $mu\sin\alpha$ Ns vertically upwards
6 (i) 14 kg
 (ii) 140 N perpendicular to sail; 280 N
7 (ii) $0.6R$
 (iii) $(0.6)^n R$
 (iv) $2.38R$ m
8 (i) 8.84 m
 (ii) 0.2 s, $\begin{pmatrix} 5 \\ 6.7 \end{pmatrix}$ms^{-1}, $\begin{pmatrix} -3 \\ 6.7 \end{pmatrix}$ms^{-1}
 (iii) 1.54
 (iv) 4.70 m
9 (i) $\begin{pmatrix} 2.5 \\ -3.96 \end{pmatrix}$ms^{-1}
 (ii) 1.01 m
 (iii) 1.41 m
 (iv) $(0.7)^n \times 2.02$ m
 (v) 7

10 (i) 24.8°; 60° to cushions
 (ii) 1.6 ms^{-1}
 (iii) arctan $(e\tan\alpha)$, $(90 - \alpha)°$ to cushions; eu, e
11 (i) 2.375 m
 (ii) 1.73 m, 0.65 m
 (iii) 52.8°

Chapter 7

? (Page 143)

A triangle is a rigid shape; for given sides, angles are fixed.

? (Page 144)

Tension: AE, ED, BE, CE
Compression: AB, CD, BC.

Experiment (Page 148)
(i) AB, FG and ED are in tension; other rods are in compression.
(ii) AB, FG and ED.
(iii) AB: 0.49 N; BC: 0.28 N, BF, FC, FG and CG: 0.57 N; CD: 0.85 N; DG: 1.70 N; EF: 1.47 N.

Exercise 7A (Page 148)
1 (i) 1000 N, 1000 N
 (ii)

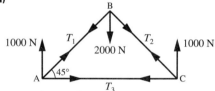

 (iii) negative tension
 (iv) $-1000\sqrt{2}$, 1000
 (v) $-1000\sqrt{2}$
 (vii) AB, BC, $1000\sqrt{2}$ N (C), AC, 1000 N (T)
2 (i) 540, 960
 (ii)

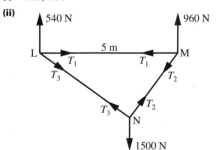

 (iii) $T_1 + 0.6T_2 = 0$, $S_2 - 0.8T_2 = 0$, -720, 1200
 (iv) 900
 (vi) 720 N (C), 1200 N (T), 900 N (T)
3 (i) 200 N, 100 N, 100 N
 (ii) 200 N (T), 200 N (T), $100\sqrt{3}$ N (C).

4 (i) 577 N

  (ii) (a) 577 N, 500 N

   (b) 764 N, 40.9° to horizontal

  (iii) 577 (T), 577 (C) 289 (C)

5 (i) A: −1000 N, C: 3000 N (vertically up)

  (ii) AB: 2000 N (T), BC: $2000\sqrt{3}$ N (C),
   AC: $1000\sqrt{3}$ N (C)

6 Horizontal rod: 1443 N (T), others 1443 N (C).

7 AE, BC: $5000\sqrt{3}$ (C); AD, BD: $1000\sqrt{3}$ (T);
  ED, CD: $2500\sqrt{3}$ (T); AB: $3000\sqrt{3}$ (C)

8 AE: 3175 N (C); AB: 2598 N (C); BC: 6062 N (C);
  CD: 3031 N (T); DE: 1588 N (T); AD: 2021 N (T);
  BD: 866 N (C)

9 PT, SR: 462 N (C); PQ, QR: 231 N (T);
  TS: 231 N (C); TQ, QS: 0

10 (i)

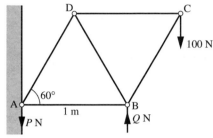

A: 50 N ↓, B: 150 N ↑

(ii)

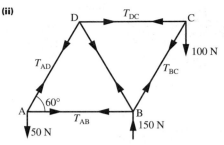

(iii) BC: $200\dfrac{\sqrt{3}}{3}$ N (C), CD, AD: $100\dfrac{\sqrt{3}}{3}$ N (T),
  AB: $50\dfrac{\sqrt{3}}{3}$ N (C), BD: $100\dfrac{\sqrt{3}}{3}$ N (C)

11 (i)

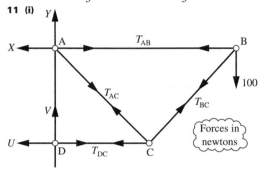

(iii) −200

(iv) CD: 200 N (C), BC: $100\sqrt{2}$ N (C), AB: 100 N
  (T), AC: $100\sqrt{2}$ N (T)

Index